Make More Money With Your Skills

Unlock Your Mental Potential
To Grow Your Business By
Creating Passive Income That
Will Change Your Life

Kenneth C. Lorenz

This book is dedicated to all the great and fantastic readers out there and to those who are eager to know how to increase their memory and unleash the power of their minds,
Thanks.

Table of Contents

Know Your Brain

To

Improve Your Memory

Improve Your Concentration
To Be More Productive

Kenneth C. Lorenz

This book is dedicated to all the great and fantastic readers out there and to those who are eager to know how to increase their memory and unleash the power of their minds,
Thanks.

INTRODUCTION

Living beings that have a nervous system are capable of modifying their behavior as a result of learning. Memory is a psychological process that allows us to keep different elements of information up to date while we integrate them. It is the retention in the time of the information learned. This retention depends on inner mental illustrations and the ability to revive and make present such illustrations. Not all pictures are memory; for this, they must come from learning.

Studies conducted in cognitive memory psychology and cognitive memory neuroscience designated distinctive memory frameworks in the human cerebrum, each with its characteristics, functions, and processes. We can characterize memory as the mental cycle used to encode information, store it in our brain, and recollects it when the person needs it. The important thing is that this information acquired through learning can be retrieved when necessary, sometimes with great speed and precision and sometimes with incredible difficulty.

Memory is a psychological process used to store information encoded. This information can be retrieved, sometimes voluntarily and consciously and sometimes involuntarily. In the investigation of memory, a few specialists have highlighted its structural components while others have focused on memory processes.

The essential thing for any human being is their ability to store experiences and benefit from their future performance experiences.

The gears and mechanisms that govern the functioning of this colossal psychological process work with such a degree of perfection that the healthy person is hardly aware that all his actions and all his verbal communication depend on the correct functioning of his memory. However, when memory fails, either circumstantially or permanently, the individual realizes its importance amid frustration.

Information can be retrieved, sometimes voluntarily and consciously and other times involuntary. In memory studies, researchers have highlighted its structural components while others have focused on memory processes. Possibly the most essential thing for any human being is their ability to store experiences and benefit from these experiences in their future performance.

HUMAN MEMORY

Memory is the brain's ability to retain information, that is, to assimilate, retain and recall, in the form of memory, the information learned during the experience or through the senses. From this, we may presume that the ability to learn and store the acquired data makes possible the knowledge on which all our subjective actions and social behaviors depend, precisely based on the recovery at the level of awareness of the information previously stored. Memory is a brain function that enables the body to encode, garners, and restore data from the past. It arises from repetitive synaptic connections between neurons, creating neural networks (the so-called long-term potentiation).

The memory can retain past experiences and, depending on the time range; it is conventionally classified into short term memory (the result of simple excitation of the synapse to reinforce or sensitize transiently), medium memory term and long-term memory (the result of a permanent strengthening of the synapse thanks to the activation of some specific genes and the synthesis of the corresponding proteins). The hippocampus is the piece of the brain related to memory and learning. An example supporting the aforementioned is Alzheimer's disease, which attacks the hippocampus's neurons, causing the person to lose memory and not remember their relatives on many occasions.

To understand the hippocampus, we need to start the process of processes at different levels that human beings relate to in their daily lives; we need to change habits, for example, to be disciplined in reading, writing, and reflecting; I must say that this process requires a lot of patience, and also that we like what we are doing, have a love for reading, writing, and reflection, and have courage with ourselves. Interest and this must be day after day, for many years, until this habit is deeply anchored in our interior and especially in the hippocampus, in such a way that, afterward, we are not going to battle because our body is exercised, our mind and our cognitive-consciousness. And we also need to eat high-quality food, for example, fruits and vegetables, white meats such as chicken and fish, eat seeds, walnuts, almonds, peanuts, sunflower seeds, and drink two liters of water daily, to start the process of increasing memory.

In practical terms, memory (or, better, memories) is the expression that learning has

occurred. Hence, memory and learning processes are challenging to study separately.

The study of memory tends to focus mainly on hominids since they have the most complex brain structure on the evolutionary scale. However, the study of memory in other species is also essential to find neuroanatomical and functional differences and discover similarities. Animal studies are also usually carried out to discover the evolution of memory capacities and experiments where it is impossible to work with human beings due to ethics. Animals with a simple nervous system can acquire knowledge about the world and create memories. Of course, this ability reaches its highest expression in humans. A standard adult individual's human brain contains about 100 billion neurons and about 100 billion interconnections (synapses) between them. Although no one knows for sure the brain's memory capacity, since there is no reliable way to calculate it, estimates vary between 1 and 10 terabytes.

According to Carl Sagan, we can store information in our minds, equivalent to 10 billion encyclopedia pages. There is no single physical place for memory in our brain. Memory is scattered across different particular areas. While memories of our earliest adolescence are stored in some areas of the temporal cortex, the significance of words is stored in the central region of the right hemisphere and the learning data in the parietal-temporal cortex. The frontal lobes are dedicated to organizing perception and thinking. Many of our automatisms are stored in the cerebellum. The first studies on memory began in the field of philosophy and included techniques to improve memory. In the early centuries, memory became the quintessential paradigm of cognitive psychology. In modern decades it has become one of the main pillars of a branch of science known as cognitive neuroscience, an interdisciplinary nexus between cognitive psychology and neuroscience.

Baddeley's Model of Working Memory

Alan Baddeley and Graham Hitch (1974) were the first to introduce the concept of working memory. Their model is modular: the information enters a module, the processing is done there, and the info leaves it. The story is broken down: a car honking is the horn's sound in one module, the car's image in another. In the same way that visual processing can be conceptualized in a modular fashion, some networks deal with the orientation of lines, others with luminescence or color, or even spatial frequency, with the outline. This type of model is also called the box model [archive].

The three components of the Baddeley and Hitch's model are:

The Phonological Loop (BP): it can retain and manipulate information in the phonological form.

The Visuospatial Notebook (CVS): is loaded with information encoded in visual form.

The Central Administrator: attention mechanism of control and coordination of the slave systems (phonological loop and visuospatial notebook). It merges the information from the two subsystems and puts them concerning the knowledge kept in long-term memory. Baddeley's model does not specify this central administrator, but Baddeley, in his 1996 book, stipulates that it is similar to the Supervisory Attentional System of the Shallice and Norman model.

Subsequently, a fourth component was added to this model: the episodic buffer. At this buffer level, the central administrator can consolidate information from sensitive prints (from subsystems) and long-term memory.

This working memory division helps explain dual-task experiments, which is a paradigm developed by Baddeley himself. In these experiments, a subject is asked to process information from several sources in working memory simultaneously. For example: riding a motorbike while reciting a poem, reciting a poem while writing.

In his first such experiment, Baddeley used several groups of subjects. They had to memorize the information presented on a screen and recall it a few seconds later. The first group of residents saw only words on the screen; the second saw square icons whose color he had to name; the third saw both heroes and stories and had to pronounce either the colors or the words displayed. The different groups did not show the same performance on this test: group 1 was able to memorize about seven stories, group 2 was able to learn four icons, and group 3 was able to recall about seven words and four icons.

This observation does not go in the direction of a unitary short-term memory (since, depending on the type of word or icon information, the performance is not the same), with a fixed limited capacity. To explain this kind of observation, Alan Baddeley and Graham Hitch put forward a model containing several short-term memories.

Memory Phenomena

1. **Reminiscence**

Reminiscence consists of the total recovery of different stimuli each time we memorize and is described by cumulative memory. This information can come from semantic memory, which is the record of our linguistic and "encyclopedic" knowledge, as in our example of Baroque composers. The information may be in episodic memory, which is our autobiographical record, such as when we remember how many libraries, cafes, bars, etc., we have recently visited. For example, when a group of alumni meets years after graduation, they typically evoke classmates and teachers from their episodic memory. Equally typical is that, with each attempt, the list that a person recalls differs slightly; that is, you don't remember the same names every time. Reminiscence occurs because

there is continual variability in the sampling of stimuli from our memory.

2. **Hypermnesia**

Compared with reminiscence, hypermnesia is a less frequent phenomenon. It consists of obtaining increases in net memory, either between successive attempts or between experimental groups. To produce hypermnesia, statistically, we must receive significant accumulations. For this reason, hypermnesia is considered another instance of increases in memory; in this case, increases in the net recall. Finally, we can observe reminiscence without hypermnesia, but there will also be reminiscence whenever we obtain hypermnesia.

Phenomena of Our Memory

Our memory is very complex, and in many cases, it shows us how interesting it can be how we encode or remember our experiences. We will discuss some fascinating phenomena about our memory:

1. We better remember what excites us.

The psychologist from the University of California Gazzaniga, tells us that two characteristics favor an experience being stored in our memory:

1st: We remember better facts associated with emotions or intense emotional states. If we try to remember an event near or far in time, we will quickly realize that most of the experiences that come to mind are related to situations or events that moved us somehow. We better remember special moments, both joyous and painful.

2nd: Those events that surprise us or make us curious are also recorded in our memory. When we are surprised or curious, our brain is more predisposed to learn, it stores information related to events that surprise us, and even in this state, we are also capable of memorizing details that a priori do not interest us immensely, as has been shown in a recent study.

2. Our state of mind determines what we memorize and remember.

In the 70s, the famous cognitive psychologist Gordon H. Bower researched how we store and retrieve memories depending on the state of mind. In one of the tests, we asked a group of people to memorize lists of words going through different moods. Then, their differences were observed when remembering these words, while they also went through other states of mind.

In this way, he tended to remember memorized elements more efficiently in a state of mind, similar to what we have when evoking them.

This phenomenon is known as "mood-congruent processing," or "processing congruent with mood, "and shows us the close relationship between memory and emotion. You can expand this information by visiting this article.

3. Our brain stores the most relevant, and the mind invents the details.

Schacter, a psychologist at Harvard University, found that we change our memory every time we remember. Each time we relive a specific memory, we create some variations on the initial memory. It is as if we were somehow overwriting the memory. It seems that only major or shocking events are recorded and stored in our brains. However, the details are not so well encoded, so we add or invent them unconsciously every time we remember.

This phenomenon is an exciting strategy that our brain uses for adaptive purposes. Store only what is relevant to a lived experience, saves energy, and avoids cluttering the memory with trivial details.

4. When we have positive thoughts, the brain is responsible for generating positive emotions.

This conclusion was obtained from different studies that related the valence of thought (positive or negative) with the emotions or moods that the subjects experienced. In one study, participants were asked in a neutral situation to think about negative experiences. Under these conditions, we observed that we inhibited the brain's areas responsible for regulating emotions through neuroimaging techniques. The consequence, in some cases, is that the subjects re-experience the feelings related to memory.

On the contrary, when they were asked to imagine festive events, those same brain areas were coordinated and activated to generate pleasant emotions more easily.

In short, these studies provide us with data to conclude that our memory induces us to be optimistic since it is easier for us to generate a positive than a negative state of mind through the recall of past experiences.

5. Others can manipulate our memory.

Today we know that memory does not faithfully show us what the past has been like but instead helps us have a personal conception of the events that have occurred for adaptive and learning purposes. There are countless studies on how memory generates so-called "false memories" through, for example, conversations with other people. Specifically, there is a study that I find especially interesting:

It consisted of showing the participants individually ten photographs in which they appeared, when they were children, on a family trip, on an excursion, or on a special occasion. They did not know that one of those photos was not real; it was a montage. The participants had to give details about what had happened that day and talk about everything they remembered concerning the photograph and the situation in which they took it. Curiously, the vast majority of people remembered many things from that "fictitious day"; they even gave precise details about what had happened in some situations that involved the moment of photography. This shows us the capacity to generate unreal memories and how memory can adapt to find coherence with our knowledge.

Many studies show us how, in certain situations or conditions, our memory is incredibly malleable. The hypnosis clinic has been used for decades to find specific memories in the minds of

clinical subjects. Nowadays, it has been seen that these techniques enhance memory, but also the ability to generate false
memories, which is why they are no longer used for this purpose.

Suggestive techniques and, more specifically, clinical hypnosis are shrouded in innumerable myths, but they are potent strategies at a therapeutic level, in the right professionals' hands. But in the field of regressions, it has proven ineffective.

The Memory from the Point of View of Psychology

Study a little the relationship between memory and psychology. Memory psychology tells us that we have to engage them with memory to remember events, events, or processes. The way toward shaping a memory includes encoding, putting away, holding, and later reviewing data and past encounters.

Cognitive psychologist Margaret W. Matlin expressed memory as the "cycle of holding data after some time." Others have characterized it as the capacity to utilize our previous encounters to decide our future way.

When asked to define memory, most people think of studying for a test or remembering where we put our car keys. However, memory is essential in our daily life. We could not function in our day-to-day or advance without trusting our memory.

The way toward encoding a memory starts when we are conceived and happens consistently. For something to turn into a memory, it should initially be gotten by at least one of our faculties. Memory begins in short-term storage. We learn how to buckle our shoes, for instance. When we have the procedure absorbed, it enters our long-term memory, and we can execute it without deliberately considering the means in question.

Significant memories often move from short-term memory to long-term memory. We can do transfer information to long-term memory for durable storage in several stages. Data can be fixed in long-term memory through recurrence, like preparing for a test or taking steps repeatedly until moving can be done mechanically, or associate it with other recently obtained information, for example, recalling another colleague by partner their name with a picture.

Motivation is another element to consider since information related to something you have a great interest in is predictable to be stored in your long-term memory. This is why some people may remember their favorite baseball player's statistics long after they retired or remember when they bought their favorite pair of shoes.

Usually, we are not conscious of what is in our memory until we need that information. We then use the recovery process to move it to the fore when we need to utilize it. Again, most of this process happens without focusing on it, especially with everyday tasks, but other kinds of memories require more exertion to bring to the fore.

Memory loss is frequently allied with aging, but several factors can trigger short-term and long-term memory loss, such as injuries, medications, and proving a painful happening.

Divide Memories into Types and Study the Mechanism

There are different types of memories. In cognitive psychology, an area of study that looks at how the memory mechanism works, a phone number you've temporarily memorized, and the knowledge that if you dial 117, you will hear a recording of the current time, different types of memories are considered. The first is known as "short-term memory" and the second as "long-term memory." This disparity is made because it is hypothesized that these types of memory have different mechanisms, or, in other words, that they have various agencies operating in the background. Taking as an example short- and long-term memory, based on direct experience, it may seem that the temporary memorization of something and the permanent use of acquired knowledge is done with different mechanisms. However, as I said, this is only a working hypothesis, and one cannot simply assume that these two types of memory have other agencies.

Even when it comes to the division between short and long-term memory, the debate started a long time ago and continues today. Giving two different explanations for these two types of memory remains the standard approach in cognitive psychology textbooks (Atkinson and Shiffrin, 1968). However, on the other hand, recent research takes a negative view of this hypothesis and suggests that it might be possible to explain them with a single mechanism (Russo & Grammatopoulou, 2003). There are strong arguments both for the view that the distinction between short and long-term memory is necessary and for the idea that it is not.

Change Perspective? Change Direction? More Divisions

If there is a long-standing debate that cannot be resolved, it is likely essential to reconsider how we approach the problem. It's necessary to think of things from a new or a different angle, and here is also the method for making more detailed distinctions. it could also describe it as "putting things in order." There are different types of memory because someone distinguished them, but that doesn't necessarily mean that what hasn't been indicated is all the same. There are cases where the types of memory that must be considered separately get mixed up.

I realized an "article memory" and an "order memory" in the temporary memory through my research. Imagine that the words appear one after the other on a screen and that you have to memorize both the words and the order in which they appear. To repeat the words in the order in which you remembered them, you must recognize both the stories themselves (called "item") and their order. This is called a "serial recovery task," It is one of the tests with simplified conditions that we use to facilitate memory study. What if we tried to separate the article memory and the control memory? While the idea that element memory and control memory have different mechanisms has been proposed in the past (Bjork and Healy, 1974; Toga and Hoshino, 2012; Toga, Moru and Hoshino, 2010), it does not 'had never been introduced. in the debate on the need to distinguish between short- and long-term memory.

After carrying out several experiments, we obtained results that cannot be explained without making assumptions regarding the command memory, at least two mechanisms, one based on phonemic information which can only be used for a short time and another that relies on another nice one. Information is unrelated to sound (Toga & Hoshino, 2015). It isn't known whether this is the case concerning element memory. Therefore, at least for now, in the case of control memory, it seems preferable to assume a functional distinction between short-term and long-term memory.

The Mechanism of Memory Is Part of The Means of The Mind.

In addition to dividing memory into types, it is also essential to examine the possibility that the types of memory that have been distinguished may work with the same background mechanism and how these different memory types are related to each other. And when it comes to those relationships, we shouldn't limit our research to memory. In recent years, the leap forward in memory studies has been made possible by moving from a concept of short-term memory as simple information storage to a picture of "working memory" that emphasizes the link between short-term memory and cognitive information processing is involved in activities, such as reasoning, comprehension and language learning

(Baddeley 2012; Baddeley & Hitch, 1974). In this dissertation project, we also focus on the factors that affect this working memory. Memory is involved in various works of the mind.

Understanding the mechanisms of memory, let alone the mind's tools, takes a lot of time and effort. Scientific advances today are incredible. To avoid a future in a hundred or two hundred years where we understand everything.

Types of Psychological Memory

While expertise has a different explanation for short-term memory, it is commonly defined as remembering things that happened promptly for up to a couple of days. In general, it is approved that five to nine details can be kept in short-term active memory for easy retrieval. Patients suffering from short-term memory loss cannot remember who entered a place five minutes earlier, but they can recall their childhood friend from 50 years ago.

The Different Types of Memory.

1. **Short-term-memory:** Short-term memory, also called primary or active memory, is the information that we are currently aware of or that we are thinking about. The short - term memory (MCP), also known as "primary memory" or "working memory," is the capability to

put in mind actively a small amount of information so that it is immediately available for a short period weather. The details found in short-term memory comes from paying attention to sensory memories. Most of the data stored in short-term memory will be stored for approximately 20-30 seconds, but it might take a couple of moments if the information is not actively held. Some information can last in short-term memory for up to a minute, but most information decays spontaneously quite quickly.

2. **Sensory memory:** Sensory memory is the shortest-term memory element. It is the capacity to hold impressions of tactile data after the first improvements have finished.

3. **Long-term memory:** Long-term memory is sufficient for storing information for a long time. Despite our everyday impressions of forgetting, it seems likely that long-term memory deteriorates gradually and can keep a seemingly limitless number of details almost for all time. Long-term memory is a crucial element to carry out our daily tasks

without errors and autonomously. This type of memory makes reference to the brain's capability to store facts, knowledge, or experience and later retrieve those memories. Long-term memory is a tremendous and complex capacity that involves a large number of brain structures. For this reason, it is susceptible to brain damage. Fortunately, practice and cognitive training can improve this critical cognitive function.

Types of Long-Term Memory

- **Declarative memory:** It is the details kept in our memory that we can verbally account for. The brain's portion with which they are related is the medial temporal lobe, the diencephalon, and the neocortex.

It is subdivided into two;

1. **Semantic memory:** It is the arrangement of data that we have about our general environment. This information is distinct from the learning episode. It includes our vocabulary, our academic knowledge, or what we know about each concept. For example, we know that the apple is a fruit that can be eaten, that it can have different colors, that it comes from the

apple tree, but we possibly don't recollect when we learned all this information.

2. **Episodic memory**: It includes the memory of the concrete events we have experienced, with an intense relationship with the learning episode. For example, I remembered what we ate yesterday, where we parked the car, when we earlier visited a new city, who went to a party last year, or when we met someone.

- **Non-declarative memory**: It is the type of information that we store in our memory but about which we "cannot speak" as such. It is mostly merged through inexplicit learning (we might not be aware of this learning). This kind of memory is much more opposed to brain damage, so it is usually less affected. It involves various parts of the brain, like the neocortex, amygdala, cerebellum, and basal ganglia. It is divided into two;

- **Motor or Procedural memory**: It consists of information on muscle movements that we have managed to automate through practice habits and skills. For example, I was riding a bicycle, driving, kicking a ball, or operating a computer mouse.

Information is kept in memory in an organized way through images, semantic networks, or diagrams. A semantic or propositional web is a set of significantly associated and hierarchically organized information units. However, when the number of information units is very high, the semantic network would be excessively complicated, and the schema model is preferred. A scheme is an organized structure of knowledge on a particular topic, which constitutes models that describe specific situations or information.

So, in what way is the new knowledge integrated with the information already stored in memory?

In this process, participate:

The elaboration, which consists of giving meaning to the new information, relating it to what we already have registered in our memory. Understanding occurs by integrating and comparing further details with our schematics and knowledge. Because of this, it is easier to remember the material that is prepared during learning: firstly, because it is a form of review that facilitates the information being stored in long-term memory; and secondly, because more links between knowledge are activated and established so that more routes will be available to reach them. Of course, if students elaborate on the new information by making faulty connections or misdirected explanations, all of these errors will be remembered as well.

The organization is the second processing element that enhances learning. It is easier to learn and remember well-organized material. Placing a concept in a structure will help you learn and remember general definitions and concrete examples, and when you need the information, the system will serve as a guide to find it.

The context is the third element that influences learning. Along with the information, aspects of the physical and emotional context, places, rooms, how we felt on a particular day, which was with us, etc., are learned. The recall of information will be easier if the retrieval context is similar to the original (performance improves if you study for an exam under conditions identical to those of the test).

Priming: It refers to the facilitation that occurs when we activate a concept in our brain. For example, we will likely take less time to remember the word "bird" if we have previously been talking about "birds," "sparrows," or "seagulls."

Classical conditioning: The relationship between a determined stimulant and the previously paired response with an unreserved stimulus. For example, suppose they ring a bell (conditioned stimulus) before applying a current air over our eye (unconditioned stimulus). In that case, it will be enough for us to hear the bell blink (conditioned response). This relationship would be part of the non-declarative memory.

How to Improve Long-Term Memory?

Each type of memory, such as long-term or short-term memory, can be stimulated, developed, and activated if time is spent working on them and a lifestyle with healthy habits is promoted. Different resources can contribute to a better stimulation of memory systems. How to improve long-term memory? To enhance long-term memory, it is essential to:

1.   **Stimulate the body:** many studies defend the correlation between physical exercise realization and better memory systems productivity.

2.   **A correct diet:** Besides a healthy diet, certain foods are related to increased memory activity. Some of the foods for memory are bluefish, nuts, green vegetables, and fruits (mostly red fruits and apples). However, in the same way that we find foods that help stimulate memory, there is a set of foods that damage our brain, thereby affecting memory productivity, such as foods high in saturated fat, red meat, fried foods, and junk food, sweets, and cakes, fatty cheeses and foods high in sugar or salt.

3.   **Rest:** in the same way that physical stimulation is essential for the activation of memory, the hours of rest are also necessary for its correct functioning, recommending a sleep of 8 hours a day.

4.   **Exercises to improve long-term memory:** to strengthen memory and make it more productive use, the only way is not through study; many games allow memory improvement. The two types of exercises that most promote the development, stimulation, and activation of long-term memory are concentration exercises and verbal fluency exercises.

Long-Term Memory Disorders

Occasional little oversights are not necessary. But severely impaired memory can indicate a neurodegenerative disease. Some tumors, strokes, poisonings, head injuries, or emotionally traumatic experiences can manifest with long-term memory impairment.

How Can Short-Term Memories Become Long-Term Memories?

As short-term memory is limited in both capacity and duration, memory retention requires transferring information from short-term memory to long-term memory. How exactly does this happen? There are different ways by which data can be shared with long-term memory.

Fragmentation is a memorization technique that can facilitate the transfer of information to long-term memory. This approach involves dividing the piece of information into smaller parts. If you were trying to master a string of numbers, for instance, you would separate them into three or four blocks of elements.

The essay can also help the information get into long-term memory. You can use this approach when studying materials for an exam. Rather than merely reviewing the story once or twice, you can go through your notes repeatedly until the critical information is confirmed in memory.

Causes of Memory Loss

The memory disorders related to age (called age-related memory impairment) refer to the slight physiological decline in brain function that occurs with age. Older people have some memory problems. Retrieving memories of new things, such as a new neighbor's name or how to use a new computer program, takes more time. Older people also have to practice new memories more frequently for them to be stored. People with this type of memory loss sometimes forget things, like where they left their car keys. But in them, unlike people with dementia, the ability to carry out daily activities or think is not affected. With enough time, they usually remember, although sometimes it takes longer than is convenient. This type of memory loss is not an early sign of dementia or Alzheimer's disease.

Mild cognitive impairment is a vague term used to describe alterations in mental function that are more severe than the physiological changes associated with aging but less severe than those caused by dementia. Memory loss is usually the most apparent symptom. People with mild cognitive impairment have trouble recollect recent conversations and may forget essential appointments or social events, but they often recall past events. Attention and the ability to perform usual activities are not affected. However, up to half of the people with mild cognitive impairment develop dementia in less than three years.

Dementia is a much more severe form of decreased mental function. Memory loss, particularly for newly acquired information, is often the first symptom, worsening over time. People affected by dementia can forget entire events, not just the details.

The following can happen to them:

Having trouble remembering how to do things they have done many times before and how to get to places they have been often. They are no longer being able to do things that require many steps, like following a cooking recipe, forgetting to pay bills or keep appointments and forgetting to turn off the stove, close the door of the house when they go out, or take care of a child who has been left in their care.

The Processes of Memory

Memory works through three fundamental processes.

1. **Coding:** elaborates and transforms stimuli to give them meaning. A certain level of attention is needed to carry it out, and that the trigger is relatively salient.

- **Encoding Structural**

This is the visual part of the coding; here, the information enters through the words; we can see how the words are lowercase, uppercase, short or long, without they are in italics or bold and in the same way, it also happens with the numbers, this part of the coding may belong to short-term memory since sometimes numbers and letters are not retained for long in our memory.

- **Encoding Phonetic**

Well, as its name says here, the information enters through sounds; it is how words or numbers sound; as I said before if we read (with our eyes) the comments, it is a structural encoding, but at the moment of expressing them in a voice high or listening to them is a phonetic encoding, in the same way, this is also part of our short-term memory.

- **Encoding Semantics**

This focuses on the meaning of words, generally requires a deeper processing level, and is, therefore, better for memory than phonetic and structural coding. This, unlike the other two, is part of long-term memory due to the level of learning that it leaves.

1. **Storage:** as its name indicates, it stores or archives the previously encoded information in memory. This information is archived schematically and based on categories.

2. **Recovery:** its function is to bring stored information to consciousness, either voluntarily or incidentally. It is noteworthy that the emotional state can influence the memories that can be retrieved; anxiety can relatively hinder this operation. Therefore, when we are in the middle of an exam, we do not remember the answer, and when it is finished, yes.

How Can We Measure and Evaluate the State of Our Memory?

Measuring the state of our memory is very useful, as it has crucial repercussions in academic areas (knowing if a child is going to have difficulties learning the content of the subjects or if they need some additional help), in clinical areas (knowing if patients can remember what medication to take, or if they can be carried out in their environment without assistance), in work environments (knowing if a person is going to be able to perform a specific job) and in our day-to-day lives.

Through a complete neuropsychological evaluation, we can measure memory and other cognitive abilities efficiently and reliably. Cognifit has a set of tests that evaluate some threads of memory, such as auditory short-term memory, contextual memory, short-term memory, the non - verbal memory, the memory visual short term, working memory, and recognition. For this, we utilize different tests, in light of the good Continuous Performance Test (CPT, by Conners), on the immediate and circuitous digit trial of the Wechsler Memory Scale (WMS), on the NEPSY (by Korkman, Kirk and Kemp), in the Test of Variables of Attention (TOVA), in the Memory Malingering (TOMM), in the Test of the Tower of London (TOL) and the Visual Organization Task (VOT). We also evaluate response, processing speed, labeling, visual perception, monitoring, planning, optical scanning, and spatial concept in these tests and measuring memory.

- **Sequential Test WOM-ASM:** A series of balls with different numbers appear on the screen. They will have to master the stream of numbers to be able to repeat them later. In the first place, the series will be made up of a single number, but it will progressively increase until a mistake is made. Each series of numbers will have to be reproduced after each presentation.

- **Inquiry Test REST-COM:** Objects materialize for a little time. Then you must select the word that corresponds with the images made known as soon as possible.
- **COM-NAM Identification Test:** Objects will be introduced by picture or sound. We should state what design (image or sound) the item showed up the last time or the off chance it had not recently shown up.
- **VISMEM-PLAN Concentration Test:** Stimuli will appear placed on the screen and dispensed alternately. Following an order, the impulses will show up, and a sound's appearance until the series is completed. During the presentation, pay attention to both sounds and illuminated images. In the user's turn, it will be necessary to remember the order of the stimuli' production at the right moment to reproduce them in the same order that they were presented.
- **WOM-REST Recognition Test:** Few objects showed up on the screen. First,

remember the order of showing the three items as quickly as possible. Later, four series of three things will appear, some of them different from those presented, and the initial sequence will have to be detected in the same order.

- **VISMEM Recovery Test:** Images will show on the screen for approximately five to six seconds. During that time, you have to try to recall as many objects that show in the image. After this time, the image disappears, and different options are offered, among which the user must detect the correct one.

Information Processing Theory

The approach that cognitive theories of learning begin with is information processing, which takes the computer's analogy to study and explain the human mind's workings. The mind processes information, from its input (input) to its output (output), through a series of processes (information collection, processing, storage, retrieval, and use of it when necessary) that operate successively and sequentially:

Memory is the primary process involved in such processing, and learning from this approach is the process of reception, retention, and retrieval of knowledge. Most memory models, called structural models or multistore models recognize a series of stages or sequences in information flow. Thus, information from the environment is collected in sensory memory, where it remains for a short time and passes to short-term memory, from where it can be transferred to long-term memory.

The transfer of information from one warehouse to another may decline if specific control processes are not present.

How Are Memories Formed?

You have just seen the divergent memory systems that exist. Now I'm going to explain to you how they are interrelated with each other to give memories.

When faced with an external stimulant, the first memory system put into operation is sensory memory, which is in charge of seeing the sensations and actual attributes of the stimulus we are interacting with.

The iconic memory for acknowledging visual stimuli and the echoic memory for recognizing auditory stimuli is put into operation.

The information received by sensory memory is sent to short-term memory, where it will remain quiet for a short time. So that the data is not out of mind at this point, it must be rehearsed.

Suppose we have to perform a mental task. In that case, the operative memory or working memory will enter the spot, which will execute all the necessary functions to face the demands demanded.

If the working memory is activated, the central executive, the phonological loop, and the visuospatial schedule will be activated.

If information is repeated in short-term memory, it will be transmitted to long-term memory, where it will reside permanently as a memory. In this setup, the data can be altered, as we have seen previously.

This is the path where external stimuli' information travels until it becomes memories in our memory.

Curiosities about Memory

A philosopher Hermann Ebbinghaus devoted many years of his life to studying memory, reaching fascinating conclusions.

According to this author, forgetting occurs progressively, in such a way that a few days after having studied a piece of information, you only remember a small bit of what you have learned, having forgotten most of the knowledge gained.

Definitely, in the first 24 hours, you can remember approximately 50% of the information gained; after 48 hours, you can recall 30% and, after a week, you will only remember 3% of all the information you had learned days before.

To keep away from this phenomenon, you must review the information studied to properly transfer it to long-term memory, thus preserving away from its forgetfulness and combining its studying.

Thus, it is preferable to study spaced out in time rather than studying intensively in a short period.

Some other peculiarity about memory is the **Primacy Effect** and the **Recency Effect**.

The **Primacy Effect** and the **Recency Effect** refer to what comes first, and last is more easily remembered.

People remember the beginning and end of things better, forgetting more easily the intermediate content. This can be modified if the content in between has great emotional significance for the person.

For this reason, we better remember the beginning and end of a telephone conversation, a reading, a song, a movie.

Factors That Negatively Influence Memory

It is known that lack of exercise, extreme mental passivity and chronic lack of sleep, thyroid problems (metabolic), smoking, and stressful emotions such as depression and anxiety have debilitating effects on memory dynamics.

Factors That Positively Influence Memory

On the contrary, intellectually stimulating habits, such as reading and mental exercises, the intake of antioxidants such as green tea, vitamin B12, vitamin D, and the endorphins and de-stressing hormones that the body secretes during physical activity or sexual intercourse, have an enhancing effect on memory and mental processes. Adequate sleep and coffee intake are also among these positive influence factors.

Diseases That Affect Memory

Some diseases and pathologies affect the functioning of human memory in a range that can range from temporary amnesias, such as that suffered during a state of traumatic shock, and that recovers naturally and gradually, to degenerative diseases that corrupt memory, such as Alzheimer's disease, caused by the appearance of plaques and knots in different regions of the cerebral cortex that prevent proper synapse.

Memory Disorders

Memory disorders are all those alterations and pathologies that result in problems when encoding, storing, and retrieving information. If we can't access or lose our memories, we won't know where we are or who we are. Therefore, memory is a fundamental cognitive process for a human being. Hence, memory disorders can be devastating.

The primary memory disorders are amnesias.

There are several types: those that prevent storing new memories and those that contain access to memories.

Amnesias

It means memory deficit; it is the total or partial loss of memory. It can be reversible or irreversible and can affect the phase of fixing, storing, and retrieving information.

General description

Amnesia involves the loss of memory, for example, of events, information, and experiences.

While forgetting one's identity is a standard plot device in movies and television, it is not often the case with amnesia in real life.

In contrast, people with amnesia (also known as "amnesic syndrome") often know who they are. However, they may have difficult time incorporating new information and generating new memories.

Amnesia can be the consequence of damage to regions of the brain that are essential for processing memories. Unlike a short-term episode of memory loss (transient global amnesia), amnesia can be permanent.

There is no particular treatment for amnesia, but memory enhancement techniques and counseling can help people with amnesia and their families' cope.

1. **Fixation amnesia:** is the inability to consolidate new memories. When a person suffers this kind of amnesia, it is said that they "live in the present," that they will not remember anything about their past. Within this type are the "anterograde amnesias." Anterograde amnesias are always organic in origin and occur as a consequence of a neurological event.

2. **Conservation amnesia:** It is the inability to remember something. A loss of memories of those already stored. Not all memories have the same ease of being forgotten.

Ribot's law says those memories more recent, less organized, and less automated; they are more vulnerable to being lost. There are different types of conservation amnesia.

- **Global:** A person can lose all the memories of his past.
- **Lacunar:** The memories that are lost are delimited in time.
- **Selective:** They are divided into two types:
- **Episodic:** a specific life event is forgotten.
- **Semantics:** what is lost is knowledge or certain types of experience.

3. **Evocation amnesia:** Amnesia memories forget the memory. When the memory is not lost, it isn't easy to bring it to remembrance when the person does not remember something but has the feeling of knowing it. Perhaps this may be due to an altered emotional state (high anxiety), asthenia, inattention; exposure to content

that interferes with the ability to retrieve information, etc.

Symptoms

The two main characteristics of amnesia are:

- Difficulty learning new information after the onset of amnesia (anterograde amnesia)
- Struggling to remember past events and information that used to be familiar (retrograde amnesia)

Most people have short-term memory problems and cannot retain new information. Recent memories are more likely to be lost, while more distant or deeply rooted ones are preserved. Some people can recall childhood experiences or know previous presidents' names, but they cannot say the word of the current president, they do not know what month it is, and they find it difficult to recall what they had for breakfast.

Isolated memory loss does not affect a person's intelligence, general knowledge, awareness, attention span, judgment, personality, or identity. People with amnesia can naturally understand oral and written words and learn skills such as riding a bike or playing the piano. They may realize that they have a memory disorder.

Amnesia is not the same as dementia. Dementia often means memory loss, but it also entails other major cognitive problems that lead to a lessened ability to function in daily life.

Memory loss is also a common symptom of moderate cognitive impairment, but the memory and mental problems from this impairment are not as severe as those with dementia.

Other signs and symptoms

Based on the cause of the amnesia, other signs and symptoms may include:

- False memories (collusion), invented entirely or from genuine memories misplaced in time.
- Confusion or disorientation

When to see the doctor

A person who suffers from memory loss, head injury, confusion, or disorientation for no apparent reason needs instant medical assistance.

A person with amnesia may be unable to recognize their location or have the courage to seek medical attention. If it turns out that somebody you know has symptoms of amnesia, help them seek medical attention.

Further signs and symptoms

Based on the origin of the amnesia, other signs and symptoms may include:

- Fake memories (confabulation), either ultimately invented or made up of real memories misplaced in time.
- Confusion or disorientation

When to visit a doctor

Anyone who encounters unexplained memory loss, head injury, confusion, or bafflement needs immediate medical attention.

A person with amnesia may be unable to recognize his or her location or have the presence of mind to seek medical assistance. If it turns out that someone you know has symptoms of amnesia, help the person get medical care.

Causes of Amnesias

Normal memory function includes many parts of the brain. Any disease or injury that influences the brain can affect memory.

Amnesia can cause damage the brain structures that make up the limbic system, which controls emotions and memories. These structures include the thalamus, which lies in the center of the brain, and the hippocampus's formations, which lie within the brain's temporal lobes.

Amnesia generated by brain injury or damage is called "neurological amnesia." Possible causes of neurological amnesia are:

- Stroke

- Inflammation of the brain (encephalitis) resulting from an infection by a virus, such as the herpes simplex virus, is just as an autoimmune reaction to Cancer elsewhere in the body (paraneoplastic limbic encephalitis) or as an autoimmune response in the absence of Cancer.
- Lack of adequate oxygen to the brain, for example, due to a heart attack, shortness of breath, or carbon monoxide poisoning.
- Long-term alcohol abuse leading to thiamine (vitamin B-1) deficiency (Wernicke-Kórsakov syndrome)
- Tumors in parts of the brain that sway memory
- Deteriorating brain diseases, such as Alzheimer's disease and other forms of dementia
- Convulsions: Some medications, such as benzodiazepines or other drugs, that acts as a tranquilizer.
- Head injuries that cause a shock, whether from a car or sports accident, can cause confusion and trouble memorizing new information. This is specifically common in the early stages of recovery. In general, minor head injuries do not cause long-

term amnesia, but more severe injuries can lead to permanent amnesia.

Another unusual type of amnesia, called "dissociative amnesia" (psychogenic), comes from an emotional shock or trauma, such as being a victim of a violent crime. In this disarray, a person may forget personal memories and autobiographical information, but usually only briefly.

- Concomitant Psychological Problems

Many patients with memory loss existing with other enthusiastic issues like sadness, stress, and uneasiness.

In these patients, memory loss is expected to low concentration and not observing things rather than actual memory impairment. Sleeping problems are also caused for poor memory in these patients.

- Trauma, Head Injury, Epileptic Seizure or Stroke: These can lead to memory loss or sudden amnesia. In travel, some of the blood supply to a part of the brain is cut off. This causes brain tissues to die. Suppose the patient forgets everything that happened before the incident. In that case, it is called retrograde amnesia, and if he or she forgets everything that occurred after the incident, it is called anterograde amnesia. This acute or sudden amnesia is caused due to a lack of adequate oxygen in certain parts of the brain.

Other Causes of Amnesia

Other causes of amnesia include:

Thyroid problems: those with lower thyroid gland activities are at the possibility of memory loss.

Tranquilizers and some medications used against Parkinson's disease can cause memory loss over time. Long-term damage to the brain from alcohol abuse. Korsakoff's psychosis is caused by long-term alcohol abuse.

Dietary or Other Deficiency of Vitamin B1 Or Thiamine Can Cause Amnesia:

Transient global amnesia is caused by difficulty with blood flow to part of the brain, which causes unexpected episodes of memory loss that a person cannot recall afterward.

Psychogenic amnesia: The patient blocks a part of his memory of an unpleasant action in the past. This makes them unable to remember crucial information.

Infantile or childhood amnesia: inability to recollect actions from early childhood. This may be because of psychological stress during that period of life.

Brain tumors can lead to amnesia.

Brain infections like Lyme disease, Syphilis, or HIV / AIDS can lead to memory loss.

- After certain types of neurosurgery.
- After cancer chemotherapy, brain radiation, or bone marrow transplant
- After electroconvulsive therapy, especially over the long term.
- Reduce memory decline as seen in dementia caused by Alzheimer's disease
- Memory loss can be seen in poorly controlled cases of bipolar disorder or schizophrenia.
- Hormonal changes are responsible for memory loss. For example, the risk of memory loss rises with lower estrogen levels in women after menopause. The elderly with corticosteroid levels are at risk for memory impairment.
- General physical illness can affect concentration and memory.

Risk factors

Your chances of having amnesia may be increased if you have:

- Brain surgery, head injury, or trauma
- Stroke
- Excessive alcohol consumption
- Convulsions
- Complications

- Amnesia varies in severity and extent, but even mild amnesia can affect daily activities and life quality. The syndrome can cause problems at work, school, and in social settings.
- You may not be able to retrieve lost memories. Some people with acute memory problems need to live in a supervised setting or a long-term care facility.

Prevention

Since damage to the brain can cause amnesia, it is essential to take steps to minimize the chance of brain injury. For example:

- Avoid drinking alcohol in excess.
- Wear a helmet when biking or a seat belt when riding.
- Treat any infection quickly, so it has no chance of spreading to the brain.
- Seek instant medical treatment if you have symptoms that put forward a stroke or brain aneurysms, such as a severe headache, numbness in one side, or paralysis.

Amnesic Syndrome

It is a memory disorder but without behavioral or cognitive impairment.

Korsakoff-Wernicke syndrome

Its main characteristics are:

- Antegrade (fixation) and partial retrograde (conservation) amnesia.
- Spatial and temporal disorientation.
- Confabulation (a mixture of true and false memories).
- False recognition.

This syndrome appears due to prolonged alcohol consumption and a diet deficient in thiamine or vitamin B1. In this memory disorder, only memory is affected, without more, in contrast to the other syndrome produced by alcohol, alcoholic dementia, where cognitive parts are also affected.

Pseudo amnesia

People with this memory disorder have the feeling that they have lost their memory, but objectively there is no such loss. Agnosia, for example, is sensory amnesias. Something that you see, touch, smell, etc., is not recognized. This type of amnesia is organic in origin.

Hypermnesia

It is a memory disorder in which the subject can evoke or retain an extraordinarily high amount of information.

For example, an oversized episodic memory with an inability to forget memories of one's own life, which interferes with the clarity of the individual's, thought. Some examples would be:

The wise idiot phenomenon: usually, these are people with autism or mental retardation characterized by learning data without apparent sense that they repeatedly repeat.

Ecmnesia: The person takes memories of his past as if they were occurring in the present moment. For instance, a mother whose child has died and gets up in the morning prepares breakfast for her deceased child.

Autobiographical panoramic vision: People who have lived it express it as my whole life passed me in front of my eyes. Exposition in detail of the subject's autobiography in a state of danger of death, moments of altered consciousness, or hypnotic trance.

Par amnesias

They are memory disorders that are characterized by the distortion of memories.

Confabulations: A mixture of true and false memories. The person reports things that have not happened, trying to compensate for the memory loss regarding what they want to remember.

Main features:

- Inventions are going to be short-lived.
- The patient expresses the supposed event without thinking about it; a process of preparation is lacking.
- This anomaly can be easily provoked, given its propensity to manifest itself.
- Once confronted with the non-existence of such events, the subject does not continue to maintain the reality of his inaccurate descriptions.
- The content of the conspiracy is usually related to the patient's usual occupation.
- The collaboration is due to organic processes in the brain.
- Retrospective falsifications (music illusions): extreme exaggeration of memories that the person has.

- False delusional memories: the person recovers a delusional idea before its appearance. The subject is hysterical about a memory.

Fantastic pseudology (mythomania): people who make up stories that many times live. They are done for something; to attract attention to you, stand out, gain personal prestige, etc. The person tells a story of things that have happened to him. They usually invented plausible things, but when the subject is confronted with reality, he recognizes them.

Possessing it on the tip of your tongue: having the subjective certainty that what you want to remember is in your memory, but you don't know it. It may be due to interference with recovery.

Checkup: when the person checks if he has done a routine task, he does not clearly remember if he has done it.

Dissociative disorders
Those memory disorders in which dissociation occurs (structured separation of mental processes that usually appear integrated). They never have an organic cause, and they are all psychogenic.

General description
Dissociative disorders involve disconnection and continuity between thoughts, memories, environments, actions, and identity. A person with dissociative disorders escapes reality in unhealthy and involuntary ways, causing problems with daily functioning.

Dissociative disorders usually appear in reaction to trauma and help keep difficult memories in check. Symptoms, which can range from amnesia to alternate identities, depend, in part, on the type of disorder you have. Periods of stress can temporarily worsen symptoms, making them more noticeable.

Treatments for dissociative disorders may include talk therapy (psychotherapy) and medications. While treating dissociative disorders can be difficult, many people learn new ways to cope and lead healthy and productive lives.

It is originated from a traumatic or extraordinarily stressful event that prevents the subject from remembering vital information. Thus, a memory gap is created. It can span from hours to decades of a person's life.

Symptoms

- Signs and symptoms based on the kind of dissociative disorders you have, but they can include:

- Memory loss (amnesia) of particular periods, events, people, and personal information
- The feeling of being separated from yourself and your emotions
- The perception that people and things around you are distorted or unreal
- A confused sense of identity
- Significant stress or problems in your relationships, your work, and other principal aspects of your life
- Lack of ability to cope well with emotions or stress.

- Mental health complications, such as depression, anxiety, suicidal thoughts, and behaviors.

There are three major dissociative disorders explained in the Diagnostic and Statistical Manual of Mental Disorders (DSM-5) issued by the American Psychiatric Association:

1. **Dissociative amnesia:** the major symptom is memory loss that is more serious than normal forgetfulness and cannot be justified by a disease's existence. You cannot remember information about yourself or events and people in your life, especially those related to a traumatic moment. Dissociative amnesia can be specific to events that occur at a particular time, such as intense fighting, or, less frequently, it can be a complete loss of memory about you. Sometimes it may involve moving or wandering in a confused state that takes you away from your life (dissociative fugue). The episode of amnesia usually comes on suddenly and can last for many years.

2. **Dissociative identity disorder**

This disorder, previously called "multiple personality disorder," is distinguished by "alternating" different identities. It is a rare memory disorder that can begin in childhood but does not attract attention until later. It is diagnosed more in women who have suffered abuse since childhood over the years. It is possible that you feel the presence of two or more people speaking or living in your head and that you feel that these identities possessed you. Each identity can have a name, a personal history, and unique characteristics, including noticeable differences in voice, gender, relationships, and even physical qualities, such as wearing glasses. There are also differences in the familiarity of each identity with the others. People with dissociative identity disorder generally also have dissociative amnesia and often experience dissociative fugue. Once established, the condition lasts for life if there is no treatment.

3. **Depersonalization-derealization disorder**

This disorder involves a continuous or episodic feeling of disconnection or of being outside of yourself, observing your actions, feelings, thoughts, and yourself from a distance as if you were watching a movie (depersonalization).

Other people and things around you may appear distant, fuzzy, or dreamlike, time may go by slower or faster, and the world may seem unreal (derealization). You may feel depersonalization, derealization, or both. Symptoms, which can be deeply distressing, may last only a few moments or come and go over the years.

Dissociative fugue
There is a loss of memory and a flight from the situation that creates discomfort. Sometimes they don't remember how they got to a place or who they are; others, yes. The person has no interest in finding out how or why he got there because he was trying to flee.

It usually appears in adulthood, but it is rare for it to appear after 50 years. If it has suffered at age 20, it may seem at 50, but it does not appear except in infrequent exceptions if it happens at this age. When it returns to its original state, before the memory disorder, the person remembers the experience after the escape, not the last thing.

Causes
Dissociative disorders often manifest as a way of coping with trauma. Most of the time, the diseases occur in children subjected to emotional

abuse, sexual abuse, or physical abuse for a long time, or, less frequently, to a frightening or highly unpredictable home environment. The stress of war or a natural disaster can lead to dissociative disorders.

Personal identity is still in the making during childhood. Therefore, a child has a greater capacity than an adult to detach from himself and observe the trauma as if it were happening to another person. A child who learns to dissociate to overcome a traumatic experience may use this coping mechanism in response to stressful situations in his life.

Risk factors
People who suffer physical, sexual, or emotional abuse in childhood for a long time are at higher risk of developing dissociative disorders.
Children and adults who go through other traumatic events, such as war, natural disaster, kidnapping, torture, or lengthy and traumatic medical procedures in childhood can also have these disorders.

Complications

People with dissociative disorders are at high risk for complications and associated diseases, such as:

- Self-harm or mutilation
- Suicidal thoughts and behavior
- Sexual dysfunction
- Alcoholism and drug abuse disorders
- Depression and anxiety disorders
- Post-traumatic stress disorder
- Personality disorders
- Sleep disorders, such as nightmares, insomnia, and sleepwalking
- Eating disorders
- Physical symptoms, such as dizziness or non-epileptic seizures
- Considerable difficulties in personal relationships and at work

Prevention

Children who are victims of physical or emotional abuse or sexual abuse are at high risk of expanding mental health disorders, such as dissociative disorders. If stress or other personal problems are influencing the way you nurse your child, seek advice.

Talk to people you have confidence in, such as a friend, your doctor, or a leader in your religious community.

Ask for help finding available means such as parenting support groups and family therapists.Attend churches and community education programs that offer parenting classes, which can also help you learn healthier parenting skills.

If your ward has been a victim of abuse or has suffered another traumatic situation, see the doctor immediately. Your doctor may mention you to a mental health specialist who can help your child recover and gain the ability to cope with challenges or situations.

1. **Bipolar Aggressiveness Mental Disorder**

Two of the multiple personalities can be adopted. There are cases where identities are complete (gait, dress, tastes, etc.). Characters can appear simultaneously (at some point, they coexist, interact, fight each other) or appear successively (first one, then another).

These personalities sometimes know each other, and sometimes they don't. If none of them is known, it is called symmetric amnesia. Another case would be asymmetric amnesia, where personality A knows B, but B does not know A. If all personalities know each other, then there is no amnesia.

One problem with this disorder is figuring out which is the primary (true) self. Some say that the primary self is the personality with the most socially acceptable characteristics.

There is also another set that thinks that this should be the personality that appears the most times. Finally, other researchers believe that the primary self should be the one that lasts the longest. When we determine the immediate self, we separate it from different personalities; we call other personalities guests.

2. Bipolar Personality Disorder

The passage from one personality to another is called a transition. It isn't easy to know which real memories are and which are not. It is a very complicated disorder, usually arising from severe traumas, appearing in the dissociation mechanism of psychological protection to the situation. It can occur in the course of other illnesses.

General description

Bipolar aggressiveness mental disorder involves sudden and repeated bouts of impulsive, aggressive, and violent behaviors or aggressive verbal outbursts in which you overreact to the situation. Road violence, domestic abuse, throwing or breaking objects, or other temper tantrums can sign intermittent explosive disorder.

These intermittent and explosive outbursts cause you great distress, negatively impact your relationships, work, and school, and can have legal and financial consequences.

Bipolar aggressiveness mental disorder is a chronic disorder that can continue for years, although the severity of outbursts may decrease with age. Treatment involves the administration of medications and psychotherapy to help you control aggressive impulses.

Symptoms

Explosive eruptions happen suddenly, with little or no warning, and typically last less than 30 minutes. These episodes can occur frequently or be separated by weeks or months of non-assault. Less severe verbal outbursts are likely to occur between bouts of physical aggression. Most of the time, you can be irritable, impulsive, aggressive, or chronically angry.

Aggressive episodes can be preceded by or accompanied by the following:

- Irritability
- Energy boost
- Racing thoughts
- Tingle
- Tremors
- Palpitations
- Chest tightness

Verbal and behavioral outbursts are oversized, and the consequences are not thought about. These may include the following:
- Tantrums
- Rants
- Heated discussions
- Screams
- Slapping, shaking, or shoving
- Physical fights
- Material damage
- Threats or attacks on people or animals

You may feel relieved and tired after the episode. Later you may feel remorse, regret, or shame.

When to see a doctor
If you recognize your behavior in describing the intermittent explosive disorder, talk to your physician about treatment options, or ask for a guide to a mental health specialist.

Causes

Intermittent Explosive Disorder may begin in childhood, after age 6, or during adolescence. It is more frequent in young adults than in older adults. The disorder's exact cause is unspecified, but it is likely due to several environmental and biological factors.

1. **Environment**: People with this disarray grew up in families where explosive behavior and verbal and physical abuse were common. Being revealed to this type of violence at an early age increases these children's chances of displaying the same traits as they mature.

2. **Genetics:** Perhaps a genetic component causes the disorder to be passed from parent to child.

3. **Differences in how the brain works:** Differences in brain structure, function, and chemistry are likely to exist in people with the intermittent explosive disorder compared to people who do not have the disease.

Risk factors

These factors increase the risk of having an intermittent explosive disorder:

History of physical abuse:

1. People who have been abused as a child or have had multiple traumatic episodes are at increased risk of sporadic incendiary disease.
2. **History of other mental health disorders:** People with an antisocial personality disorder, borderline personality disorder, or other disruptive behavior disorder, such as awareness deficit hyperactivity disorder (ADHD), are at increased risk of intermittent explosive disease.

Complications

People with intermittent explosive disorder are at higher risk for the following:

1. **They have affected personal relationships:** Often, other people think that they are always angry. You may have frequent verbal fights or physical abuse. These measures can lead to relationship problems, divorce, and family stress.
2. **Problems at work, at home, or school:** Other complications of the intermittent explosive disorder can include job loss, suspension from school, car accidents, financial problems, or legal problems.

3. **Mood problems:** Mood disorders, such as depression and anxiety, frequently happen with intermittent explosive disorder.
4. **Alcohol and other substance use problems:** Drug and alcohol issues generally occur in conjunction with the discontinuous hazardous situation.
5. **Physical health problems:** Ailments are more regular, including high blood pressure, diabetes, heart disease, stroke, ulcers, and chronic pain.
6. **Self-harm or injury:** Sometimes, intentional injuries or suicide attempts takes place.

Prevention

If you have a dangerous discontinuous problem, anticipation is likely outside your ability to control except if you receive treatment from a professional. These suggestions, combined or as part of your treatment, can help you prevent some incidents from spiraling out of control:

1. **Strictly follow your treatment:** Go to therapy sessions, practice your ability to cope with challenges or situations, and be sure to take the medications your physician prescribes, if any. Your doctor

may suggest a maintenance medication to prevent explosive episodes from coming back.

2. **Practice relaxation techniques**: Standard utilization of profound relaxing, relaxation images or yoga can help you stay still.

3. **Grow new ways of thinking (cognitive restructuring):** Changing the method you think about a frustrating circumstance using rational thoughts, reasonable expectations, and logic can improve how you see and react to an event.

4. **Use problem-solving:** Create a plan to find a way to solve a frustrating problem. Even if you can't figure it out right away, having a plan can alter your liveliness.

5. **Learn ways to improve your communication:** be attentive to the word the other person wants to communicate to you and then think of the best response you can give instead of saying the first thing that comes to mind.

6. **Change your environment:** When possible, stop or avoid situations that upset you. Additionally, organizing your time can help you better handle a

stressful or frustrating problem in the future.

7. **Avoid using substances that alter your mood:** Don't drink alcohol or use recreational or illegal drugs.

Depersonalization disorders

The person has a feeling of unreality, as if he were living a dream or as if time stopped. This disorder usually arises when someone is subjected to very intense pressure, whether in the work, academic, or social environment.

Two types are mainly distinguished:

1. **Depersonalization:** when this feeling of strangeness occurs about oneself, the body, or mental processes. The person who suffers feels like an automaton.

2. **Derealization:** when it refers to our external environment. In this case, the patient may report that he sees everything as in a movie.

General description

Depersonalization-Derealization Disorder happens when you persistently feel that you observe yourself from outside your body, or you think that the things around you are not real, or both. The feelings of depersonalization and derealization can be upsetting, and you may feel like you're in a fantasy.

Many people have an experience of depersonalization or derealization at some point in their lives. However, when these sensations continue to appear or never wholly disappear and affect your ability to function, you are considered to have depersonalization-derealization disorder. This disorder is more common in people who have had traumatic experiences.

Depersonalization-Derealization Disorder can be severe and interfere with relationships, work, and other daily activities. The primary treatment for the depersonalization-derealization disorder in communication therapy (psychotherapy), although medications are sometimes used.

Symptoms

Constant and recurring episodes of depersonalization or derealization, or both, cause distress and trouble performing at work, school, or in other particular areas of life. During these incidents, you know that your sense of disconnection is only a sensation and not a reality.

The experience and feelings of the disorder are likely to be hard to report. Panic about "going crazy" can cause you to worry about checking if you exist and determining what is truly real.

Symptoms usually begin in the mid to late teens or early adulthood. Depersonalization and derealization disorder is rare in children and older adults.

Symptoms of Depersonalization

The symptoms of depersonalization are:

- The feelings that you are an outside observer of your thoughts, feelings, your body or parts of the body, for example, as if you are floating in the air yourself
- The feeling that you are like a robot or have no control of speech or movements.
- The feeling that the body, legs, or arms appear distorted, enlarged, or shrunken, or that the head is wrapped in cotton
- Emotional or physical numbness of the senses or responses to the world around you

- The feeling that memories lack emotion and that they may or may not be your memories.

Derealization Symptoms

Derealization symptoms include:

- Feelings of being isolated or unfamiliar with the surroundings, for example, as if you are living in a movie or dream
- Feeling emotionally disconnected from the people you care about, as if you are separated from them by a wall of glass.
- An environment that appears distorted, blurry, colorless, two-dimensional, or artificial, or heightened awareness and clarity of the environment
- Distortions in the discernment of time, such as feeling that recent events are distant in the past
- Distortions of distance, size, and shape of objects
- Episodes of the depersonalization-derealization disorder can last for hours, days, weeks, or even months at a time. In some people, these episodes turn into constant feelings of depersonalization or derealization that periodically get better or worse.

When to See the Doctor

Fleeting feelings of depersonalization or derealization are standard and not necessarily a cause for concern. But constant or intense feelings of disconnection and distortion of the environment are a pointer of depersonalization-derealization disorder or other physical and mental health disorders.

See your doctor if you have feelings of depersonalization or derealization that have these characteristics:

- They upset or disturb you emotionally.
- They do not go away or are recurring.
- Interfere with work, relationships, or daily activities

Causes

The exact cause of depersonalization-derealization disorder is not well understood. Some people may be more vulnerable to depersonalization and derealization than others, possibly due to genetic and environmental factors. Heightened states of stress and fear can trigger episodes.

Depersonalization-derealization disorder symptoms may be related to childhood trauma or other situations or events that cause severe emotional stress or trauma.

Risk Factors

Features that can increase your risk for depersonalization-derealization disorder include:

- Certain character qualities that make you need to dodge or deny troublesome circumstances or make it difficult for you to adjust to them
- A severe trauma during childhood or adulthood, such as experiencing or witnessing a traumatic event or abuse
- Intense stress, such as significant relationship, financial, or work problems
- Depression or anxiety, mainly severe or prolonged depression, or concern with panic attacks
- Diversion drug use, which can trigger episodes of depersonalization or derealization

Complications

Episodes of depersonalization or derealization can be scary and disabling. They can cause the following:

- Difficulty concentrating on tasks or remembering issues.
- Interference with work and other daily activities
- Problems in the relationship with your family and with your friends
- Anxiety or depression
- Feeling hopeless

How to Keep Your Brain Fit

Your brain is truly the most beautiful part of your body. It devises creative ways to express your thoughts and emotions, coordinates movements from chopping onions to running an obstacle course, preserves your most treasured childhood memories, and solves Sunday's crossword puzzle. In any case, it's not difficult to underestimate those forces.

"Many people don't begin to think about their brain health until they notice cognitive changes and memory loss in their 60s or 70s," said Elise Caccappolo, Ph.D., associate professor neuropsychology at Columbia University Medical Center in New York City. "There are things you can do, from childhood, to keep your brain as healthy as possible throughout your life. We know that intellectual pursuit, social interaction, and perhaps more importantly, physical activity helps keep your brain sharp."

1. **Healthy heart:** The most crucial strategy, she says, is to work with your doctor to stay on top of your cardiovascular health. You want to get the blood flowing quickly through your heart and blood vessels. "High blood pressure, high cholesterol, smoking, and diabetes all increase the

risk of developing neurodegenerative diseases by barriers in blood flow to the brain," she explains. When artery walls become thick with a plaque or "harden," a condition called atherosclerosis, it is challenging to get enough blood to the brain and nourish its cells. This can also lead to ischemic stroke - when a blood clot forms in an artery, cutting off blood reservoir to part of the brain. That can cause short-term or even long-term brain damage.A healthy, energetic lifestyle will go a long way in keeping your blood flowing and avoiding those problems. A Swedish study of over 30,000 women found that those who ate healthily, exercised regularly, did not smoke, drank moderately, and kept their body mass index (BMI) below 25 had a lower risk of stroke compared to women who had none of these five had done. Goals achieved.

2. **Lots of quality sleep:** A fundamental way to keep your brain working is to turn it off for 7-9 hours a night. "Sleep is an essential thing you can do to reset the brain, let it heal, and restore mental health," said Romie Mushtaq, MD, a neurologist and integrative medicine

specialist.Research shows that during sleep, the brain removes toxins called beta-amyloids that can lead to Alzheimer's disease and other dementias. Mushtaq suggests a few simple things before going to bed.

3. **Do a digital detox:** Record the same bedtime every night and turn off all electronics and screens for at least 30-60 minutes before hitting the pillow.

4. **Leave your worries away:** Write down any problems and a quick to-do list for tomorrow to calm your brain. "Our thoughts are always racing and causing fear," she says. "But if you write it down with a pencil and paper, it tells your brain not to worry about it while you sleep."

5. **Spend time meditating:** Not only will 5-10 minutes of deep meditation soothe your mind and make it simpler to rest, but contemplation has also been appeared to decrease tension, gloom, weakness, and disarray. "Reflection can profit individuals with a sleeping disorder by causing them to nod off and stay unconscious. It likewise assists with aggravation in mind," she says. "Most

people find that not only do they sleep better, but they can concentrate better and are less anxious."

6. **Move your body:** Walking, taking dance lessons, or swimming for 30 minutes a day will help you stay slim and fit and it can also improve your cognitive health. A large Canadian study found that the more physically active adults were, the higher they scored on memory and problem-solving tests. Exercise raises blood flow to the brain and studies.

EMOTION AND MEMORY

Emotional events are remembered better than other types of events. There is a facilitating effect on memory. But what is the reason for this facilitation?

Memory is not a real copy of reality; it can be distorted or even false. Episodic memory has an affective aspect. In the classical view, memory is represented by a timeline: encoding →

consolidation → recovery. The researcher Nader added reactivation and reconsolidation to this timeline, which would allow the integration of new information on an already existing memory. The memory would therefore be relatively labile. We also know that emotional stimuli have a facilitating effect on memory.

Emotional Memory

The memory emotional refers to the ability of people to set memories from emotions. Multiple studies have revealed that the brain related to memory is closely associated with regions that modulate emotions.

Emotions are closely linked to memory, and the emotional content of events is considered to influence later memory. A lot of information acquired emotionally remembered differently than that gained neutrally.

Head and Brain Gears in Progress; think about love.

Faced with this close attachment between emotion and memory, a new memory shape has come up known as emotional memory. It is an individual human capacity characterized by developing the memory of events through the emotional impact experienced.

Memory - Emotions Relationship

Emotional memory implies that emotionally significant events are retained differently than neutral events; dynamic events are remembered better and more efficiently than more insignificant events.

Take, for example, a traumatic event during childhood, such as a car accident or a fight with a partner is frequently remembered much more specifically during adulthood than trivial events such as what you ate the previous week.

This division of memories refers to selective memory. People do not remember all information in the same way. In this sense, emotionally experienced events seem to be remembered better than the rest.

Multiple investigations show that the more significant memory of emotionally intense experiences is due to greater ease of acquisition, more extraordinary maintenance over time, and more excellent obstinance to vanishing.

Positive Emotions and Negative Emotions in Memory

Emotional memory makes a response to both positive and negative feelings. In other words, events experienced emotionally (whatever their character) seem to be remembered differently from neutral or trivial experiences.

This is because the brain structures that modulate positive emotions and those that modulate negative emotions are the same. In this way, the cerebral mechanism that explains emotional memory resides in the association, joining the feeling and memory regions' structures.

Aversive or Traumatic Events

Highly apathetic or traumatic events can cause a powerful and consolidated memory. The person can recollect these events frequently and in detail all through his life.

An example of this type of memory would be the trauma suffered during childhood, which can appear repeatedly and be remembered permanently in adulthood.

Positive Events

Discovering similes with positive emotions is somewhat more complicated. Some people can recollect in full detail the day of their wedding or their children's birth, but frequently the memory is less intense than that of adverse events.

The intensity of the emotion explains this fact. In general, adverse events cause a more significant emotional disturbance, so the feelings experienced in those moments tend to be more intense.

In this way, traumatic events can be inserted more easily into emotional memory. But this is not to say that festive event cannot. They also do so, although generally less markedly due to their lower emotional intensity. `

Brain Structures of Emotional Memory

The brain structures of emotional memory include:

1. Neuropsychology: The main brain structure responsible for carrying out memory processes and that ease memory is the hippocampus. This region is found in the temporal cortex, and it is part of the limbic system.

On its part, the brain region in charge of giving rise to emotional responses is the amygdala. This structure comprises a set of nuclei of neurons found deep in the temporal lobes and is part of the limbic system.

2. Hippocampus: Both structures (amygdala and hippocampus) are always connected. Likewise, their connection seems to have particular relevance in the formation of emotional memories.

3. Brain tonsil (blue dot): This fact puts forward the existence of two different memory systems. When people grasp neutral information (such as reading a book or learning the syllabus of a subject), the hippocampus is in charge of building the memory without the amygdala's involvement.

However, when the items to remember contain a certain emotional charge, the amygdala comes into play.

In these cases, the first memory formation occurs in the amygdala, which acts as a depository of memories related to emotional events. Hence, dynamic memory does not start in the hippocampus like other memories.

Once the amygdala has encoded the emotional element and formed the memory, it transmits the information through synaptic connections to the hippocampus, where the dynamic memory is stored.

Emotional Memory Formation Process

Experimental psychology

Emotional memory has different features and different brain registration mechanisms due to the action of emotion. The emotions prompt the information to access the brain through various structures and consolidate it more intensely.

Thus, emotional operations modify the functioning of memory, giving rise to the appearance of dynamic memory. These moderations are explained by the amygdala-hippocampus relationship and are carried out both in the coding and in the consolidation of information.

1- Emotional Coding

The first cognitive role that comes into play when shaping a memory is consciousness. Without sufficient attention, the brain cannot perceive information and store it in its previous one adequately.

In this sense, the first modification that emotions make is already detected in how the information is perceived.

Emotional responses immediately provoke an alteration in people's physical and psychological functions. When an individual experiences an emotion, both the physical and psychological elements are related to attention growth.

This certainty allows the attention given to the stimulus to be soaring so that the information is captured more quickly, and its consecutive storage is more acceptable.

2- Emotional consolidation

The second phase of emotional memory production comprises the retention or consolidation of information in the brain structures. If the knowledge gained by the senses is not consolidated in the brain, it gradually vanishes, and the memory is unremembered.

The depository of information in brain structures is not automated but rather a slow process, so it is frequently challenging to retain some detailed information in an extended period.

Nevertheless, emotional information seems to have a much shorter consolidation time. In other words, it can be stored in brain structures much more quickly.

This makes the probabilities that emotionally intense events will be recalled and maintained over time are much higher.

Influence of Memory on Emotion

The association between memory and emotion is not unidirectional but is bi-directional. This means that uniformly, emotion can influence memory (emotional memory); memory can also control emotion.

This association has been studied explicitly by neuropsychologist Elisabeth Phelps when analyzing the interaction between hippocampus and amygdala. When the hippocampus retrieves emotionally great information, it can interrelate with the amygdala to bring out the emotion that follows it.

For instance, when a person remembers a highly traumatic event, they immediately experience the event's emotions. Thus, memory can elicit emotional responses in the same way that sharing emotions can modify memory formation. The hippocampus and the amygdala are interrelated brain structures that frequently connect the emotional components to the mnestic elements.

Emotional Memory Function

The association connecting emotional structures and regions of memory is not gratuitous. The association between the hippocampus and the amygdala plays an important adaptive role.

When people are in dangerous situations, they behave with an emotional response. This response acknowledges a greater awakening of both the psychological state and the physical state of the person.

For instance, if someone visualizes that a dog will attack them, they experience an emotional response of fear. This response makes it feasible to stress the body, grow attention, and focus all the menace's senses.

By this means, the emotional response prepares the person to respond appropriately to a threat.

However, the process of defense and survival of human beings does not stop there—the brain categories the storage of emotionally intense events through the amygdala-hippocampus association to be easily remembered.

Thus, emotional memory is a human role that is similar to the survival of the species. It is much more useful for people to remember emotionally extreme elements than neutral aspects because these are usually more important.

Studies on Emotional Memory

Emotional memory works as a filter system. This is in charge of selecting the most relevant facts due to their meaning and saves them in memory in a more intense and lasting way.

From this evolutionary point of view, the human brain would correctly recall aversive experiences even when these have occurred a few times.

In this sense, Garcia & Koeling already demonstrated in 1966 that emotional memory could be formed even with a single presentation. Specifically, learning such as taste aversion or fear conditioning can be acquired with a single trial.

These experiments show a high capacity for emotional memory. This allows the formation of lasting memories exceptionally quickly and easily, a reality that does not occur with "non-emotional memory."

Other research on emotional memory has specialized in examining the mechanisms involved in the relationship between emotion and memory.

At the brain level, the structures that participate in emotional memory are the amygdala and the hippocampus. However, there appear to be more related factors.

Neuroendocrine Effects of Stress and Memory

Studies on the neuroendocrine effects of stress and its association with the origination of memories of stressful occurrences have provided appropriate emotional memory data.

When a person is put through high emotional content situations, they release many adrenal hormones. Mostly, adrenaline and glucocorticoids.

Various investigations have focused on analyzing these hormones' effect and have shown that it is closely linked to the emotion-memory relationship.

In this regard, Beylin & Shors showed in 2003 that the administration of an adrenal hormone known as corticosterone before performing a studying task regulated memory and improved memory.

Also, De Quervain revealed that the modulation of memory varies according to the moment and the intensity with which the hormones are let go. In this way, glucocorticoids make it easier for people to remember.

Subsequently, a study executed by McCaug in 2002 showed that these hormonal effects are produced through central noradrenergic mechanisms. That is, through the action of the brain amygdala.

The presence of glucocorticoids in the blood causes a greater stimulation of the amygdala. When the amygdala is active, it begins to participate directly in the formation of memories.

In this way, when these hormones are administered into the blood, memory starts to function through emotional memory mechanisms, so memory is intensified, and learning is more powerful and consolidated.

DEPRESSION AND MEMORY

Depression can develop a type of memory loss (called pseudodementia) resembling that occurring in dementia. Also, dementia usually causes depression. Therefore, determining whether dementia or depression is the cause of memory loss can be difficult. Nevertheless, people with memory loss due to depression, unlike those with dementia, are aware of their memory loss and complain about it. Also, they rarely forget important current events or personal matters. They often have other symptoms, such as intense sadness, trouble sleeping (too much or too little), slowness, or loss of appetite.

The stress can interfere with memory formation and when retrieving a memory, partly because concerns prevent the subject from paying attention to other things. However, in certain circumstances, mainly when stress is mild to moderate and does not last long, memory can improve.

When Are the Symptoms of Depression?

The subjective finding of the patient reporting memory and concentration difficulties is one of the critical symptoms for diagnosing major depression and generalized anxiety in one of the most used statistical manuals for diagnostic purposes (DSM). In patients with depression, problems concerning attention and memory are present during deflection periods (mood decay) and remission periods (disappearance of symptoms).

These difficulties present themselves in two main ways: one regarding the neurocognitive and chemical changes that accompany depression (detectable in the form of worse performance in standardized tests), the other to the distortions in thoughts about self and others, associated with deflected mood, such as negative expectations or catastrophic thinking (most noticeable during conversations or clinical interviews).

How Depression and Anxiety Can Affect Memory

Patients suffering from depression frequently complain of memory difficulties. Although people who have suffered from depression for a long time do not present, without a doubt, the memory deficits that are observed in patients with dementia, the existence of memory difficulties has interested many authors. Regarding the origin of memory problems, there is no consensus on this.

Depressed patients suffer from a lack of motivation and energy, and, as a consequence, they would record less well or recover less actively the information they receive.

Depressed patients often complain of impaired memory, attention, and concentration difficulties. These cognitive disorders are an integral part of depression.

The first studies on memory disorders in depression, dating back to the eighties, confirmed the existence of a memory deficit, both in the short and long term, the obligations being proportional to the severity of the depressive picture and disappearing with it.

Anxiety and Memory

Generalized anxiety disorder represents one of the most common anxiety disorders. It corresponds to severe anxiety, characterized by chronic cognitive disturbances such as worries or worries, for at least six months (DSM-IV). These are accompanied by psychic symptoms and somatic symptoms such as irritability, excessive health concerns, insomnia, headaches, memory, and concentration difficulties.

In chronic generalized anxiety, attention appears labile. Hypervigilance entails an exaggeration of automatic concentration and a weakening of voluntary attention that could explain the short-term memory difficulties these patients often complain about.

On the studies of anxiety and memory, we can conclude that:

- Subjects with a high level of anxiety in the testing condition use fewer resources than issues with a low level of stress.
- The effects of anxiety on performance in the different tests depend first on the availability and use of additional resources and, later on, the task's intervention on working memory capacity.

Anxiety Disorder

Although there are innate fears, most of the situations that cause us to fear daily life are learned. We put the dangerous label on problems that have caused us physical harm, which constitutes an adaptive response aimed at the survival of the person and the species. We also label the psychological threats with which we have not been able to deal adequately.

But sometimes, our brain does not respond appropriately, and everything seems dangerous. That is why the researchers believe their findings may have important implications when dealing with, for example, an anxiety disorder. Those who suffer from it are afraid of things that are not threatening at all. However, they are very limited in their daily life. According to this study, their neurons may have lost their ability to discriminate threats.

Similarly, something similar could be happening in the pros of traumatic stress disorders (PTSD). A very adverse event leaves sequelae that make the situation repeatedly relive in the face of any detail that recalls the feared situation. They can occur in soldiers, victims of sexual violence, terrorism, or natural disasters.

What Happens in The Brain of People with Anxiety?

If there is something distinctive of anxiety disorders, it is doubtlessly fear. A spread fear that produces anguish and that does not have an exact cause. Several brain areas are essential in making fear and anxiety—especially the amygdala, an almond-shaped formation, and the hippocampus.

The amygdala is in charge of alerting the rest of the brain to potential threats and activating a fear or anxiety response. The hippocampus, essential for memory consolidation and learning, is responsible for storing dangerous events in the form of memories.

In most people, the feeling of fear is adaptive, protecting us from danger. But in people with anxiety disorders, this emotion is disproportionate and, in many cases, generalized, causing great anguish that can become very limiting. It is also known that hyperactivity of the amygdala leads to the development of phobic fears.

Memory Loss from Anxiety

Anxiety has one of its most common symptoms, lack of concentration and memory loss. This cognitive difficulty leads the person to suffer a higher stress level due to the fear of forgetting appointments, conversations, people, and meaningful memories. Suffering anxiety makes it extremely difficult for us to retain information and even to be able to recover memories we already believed we had consolidated in our minds.

When memory fails us, everything fails us. When we suffer memory loss, we experience truly disconcerting and distressing moments. It is a terrifying experience that undoubtedly affects our anxiety levels even more. It is a brutal cycle in which we will only get out with professional help.

The loss of memory produced by anxiety is a clear example that, if our concern is not treated in time and correctly, in the end, it ends up affecting our cognitive structures. When anxiety becomes chronic, it ultimately affects the functioning of our brain. And it is something that can be anticipated with psychological therapy.
All this says that all anxiety has to be adequately treated since the brain is susceptible to our

lifestyle and how we face things. Mismanagement of our fears and worries will make it look resentful and long-term damaged.

Why Do These Memory Leaks Occur?

When suffering from anxiety, we realize that little by little, we are losing our memory. We are so caught up in the problems that we cannot take everything else into account. Maybe one day we will forget our house keys. Or perhaps we go to pick up our children at school. They are two examples of what we can ignore because of our anxiety.

Little by little, we will feel that we are incapable of controlling our lives. And that is part of the most distressing things we can ever feel. When we are unable to feel competent and responsible, something breaks within us.

When suffering from anxiety for a long time, the well-known hormone cortisol appears. It is a last that is released in response to a high level of stress. Its release, when normal, is even beneficial for the creation of new memories. The bad thing is when its release is constant and prolonged in time. It will be then that we begin to suffer difficulties to remember, and we will begin to suffer memory losses.

- **Cortisol damage to the brain**: When there is an excess, cortisol acts as an actual toxic. It causes the hippocampus to lose volume, and therefore memory and the expression of our emotions will be affected.
- **It hinders blood circulation in the brain:** Reduces the secretion of endorphins. It will cost us more to enjoy the things that we like and make us feel good.
- It affects sleep, whether it's insomnia or waking up continuously at night.

How to Reduce Memory Loss Due to Anxiety?

Suppose we get to the moment when we see that we are suffering from a severe memory loss. In that case, we must go immediately to the doctor's office so that he refers us to the appropriate specialists who rule out biological causes of memory problems.

Once the physical causes are ruled out, we must focus on the psychological. Anxiety is a long-term disorder that causes memory loss.

When we evaluate which is the cause of anxiety, we must treat it properly, and for this, we must:

- Let's identify stressors: We have to know how our bodies and mind react when we suffer from anxiety. For example, if the jaw is tense, if we suffer palpitations, what thoughts are presented, etc.
- We have to regain control of our life: We cannot always hide behind anxiety. We can get out of it, and we must do it as soon as possible. The responsibility is ours and ours alone.
- We can use techniques that help us relax, such as breathing exercises, physical activities, crafts, etc.
- We don't need to propel ourselves excessively hard and take life more slowly.
- We must learn again to eat well and calmly, and above all, have a good rest.

Memory Loss from Depression

As with anxiety, memory loss is one of the most common symptoms of depression. Such a neurochemical alteration occurs in the depressed brain that it can affect concentration, remembering, reacting appropriately to stimuli, or merely thinking clearly.

Those who suffer from depression do not always have to be lying in bed or on the sofa, away from reality, and leaving their day-to-day aside. That is just a cliché. It's not real. By far, most individuals with depression go about their daily tasks, and they work. Even so, depression leaves its mark on their brain function, diminishing it and hindering that person little by little.

Depression is not only a specific emotional state, but it is also an internal disorder, which produces exhaustion, apathy, and hopelessness. And if this state is prolonged in time, we will suffer a significant deterioration in our cognitive functioning.

Suffering from Depression and Memory Loss

Our mental agility will be diminished when suffering from depression. We cannot think properly. The reflexes are slow and clumsy. Memories fade, and we become distressed when we don't get immediate memories. Everything is the result of depression, and when we fall into it, we find ourselves thrown into an internal cave that takes us away from the world around us.

Memory loss from depression is more than just forgetting. It is living in a thick and dark fog that prevents us from thinking and remembering clearly. It is a very negative effect that plunges the person into absolute existential anguish and suffering a tremendous social misunderstanding. All of this will aggravate your suffering.

What Transpires in Our Brain When We Suffer from Depression?

When suffering from depression, the hormone cortisol is released in an uncontrolled way. Everything is promoted by our state of mind, worries, anguish, and pressure. This release of cortisol makes our neurons hyperactive, leading to neuronal exhaustion and even death. To reduce this neural activity, they are disconnected, and that is when problems with our mental agility begin to occur. Things are starting to be forgotten, and our ability to think is seriously impaired.

What Can We Do to Recover from Memory Loss?

Memory loss is a fact when we suffer from depression for a long time. When the depression is mild or moderate, the cognitive deficit can be reversed through therapy and memory exercises. When depression is severe or very severe, it will be necessary to combine drug therapy. Only in this way can the cognitive deficit be reduced and with-it memory loss. You can also apply treatments based on the application of vitamin complexes and diet to improve memory. All this will depend on each case and each person.

Depression, like any other psychological disorder, must be treated appropriately and as soon as possible. Wrong or no treatment can lead us to suffer from specific severe symptoms, impairing our brain structure and function.

HOW TO INCREASE MEMORY

We know that memory is related to consciousness, with the body, and Alava is associated with the human brain, the mammalian brain, and the reptilian brain; well, for the processes to start the internal exercise so that the memory begins to stimulate ourselves, we need a good diet of high quality, we need to breathe correctly, we need to get enough sleep (at least five hours), a good bath in the morning. We begin the exercises in reading and reflect on what we have read and understanding of it. For this, we need to write some keywords (the most crucial thing that seems to us about reading), and then we will make an acrostic of the keywords, and then we will develop a simple mind map, and at the end of all this, we are happy to finish doing a good concept map. If we do what we just mentioned every day, we will be successful since the hippocampus will be working day after day. The memory will have its changes and processes so that the final results will be excellent short-term, medium-term, and long-term memory and exceptional learning. You have to be very tolerant, not lose track of heart and have a mission and a vision until you reach the top.

We are getting older and stay healthy longer. Unfortunately, there are no drugs and surgeries to keep the brain healthy.

Memory contributes a lot to our lives, and thanks to her, we retain the knowledge that helps us develop ourselves properly for the world. There are simple ways to sharpen your memory and learn when to seek help for memory loss; these are;

1. Include Physical Activity in Your Daily Practices: Physical pursuit increases blood flow to the entire body, including the brain. This could help you keep your memory active.

For nearly healthy adults, the Department of Health and Human Services recommends a weekly minimum of 150 minutes of little aerobic exercise, such as brisk walking, or 75 minutes of vigorous aerobic activity, like jogging, preferably spread out over the week. If you don't have time for a standard training routine, include a few 10-minute walks throughout the day.

2. Be Mentally Active: Correspondingly, physical activity helps keep the body in shape, activities that stimulate the mind help keep the brain in shape and prevent memory loss. Do crosswords. Play bridge. Take different roads when driving—Master how to play musical instruments. Take part at a local school or community organization.

3. Get Social Regularly: Social interaction helps prevent depression and stress, putting up memory loss. Look for chances to get together with loved ones, friends, or other people, especially if you live alone.

4. Get Organized: You are more likely to forget things if your house and your notes are cluttered. Write down tasks, appointments, or other events in a special notebook, a calendar, or an electronic agenda. Perhaps repeating each entry out loud as you write it down will help you remember it. Update your to-do lists, and check off the ones you've already completed. Reserve a place to store your wallet, keys, glasses, and other essentials.

Avoid distractions and don't do too many things at once. If you focus on the information you are trying to retain, you are more likely to remember it later. It can also help relate what you are trying to maintain to a favorite song or other familiar concepts.

5. Sleep Well: Sleep is essential to help you consolidate your memories to recall them later. Make good sleep a priority. Sleeping is a necessary process, not only in the consolidation of memories but also in selecting that information that must be discarded and forgotten or in motor skills learning. Adults need like 7-9 hours of sleep per day.

6. Follow A Healthy Diet: A balanced healthy diet can be as useful for your brain as it is for your heart. Eat fresh fruits, vegetables, and entire grains. Pick low-fat protein sources, for example, fish, beans, and skinless chicken. What you drink also counts. Too much alcohol can cause uncertainty and memory loss. So can drug use.

Even more important than taking a supplement is eating unprocessed and varied foods. Brain Food's role in improving your memory is truly enormous, and I allow everyone to experience the difference for themselves.

7. Manage Chronic Conditions: Follow your doctor's treatment recommendations for medical conditions, such as depression, high blood pressure, high cholesterol, diabetes, obesity, and hearing loss. The more you deal with yourself, the better your memory will be. Also, regularly review your medications with your doctor. Various drugs can affect memory.

8. Supplements: Your brain and memory need the right nutrients to function optimally. Unfortunately, we often lack these in our

Western diet. Supplements are, therefore, an excellent way to supplement deficiencies and thus improve your cognitive functions.

Specifically, for your memory, there are nutritional supplements that combine the most crucial memory ingredients.

9. Exercises: I've said it before: your brain is like a muscle you can train to get stronger. This also applies to a brain function such as your memory. Only when you use a part regularly does your brain understand that it is needed, and energy goes into keeping the part sharp and fresh.

You can come up with the most diverse exercises to train and improve your memory. Think of buying puzzle books, learning a second language, or playing memory games. Variety is excellent because your brain likes a challenge.

10. Movement: The movement has a significant impact on cognitive functions. Think not only of your memory but also, for example, your concentration, learning ability, and consciousness. All of these cognitive brain functions require blood packed with oxygen and nutrients.

Regular exercise improves blood flow in your brain and body and, thus, your memory and other cognitive functions.

11. Keep Practicing: Good old days when you had to memorize things. Still, it is good for the brain to learn something. This keeps the brain fit. Try to remember different phone numbers or the lyrics of a song. By repeating it a lot, the information ends up in your long-term memory so that you always benefit from it. When you learn something new, new nerve connections are created that improve memory. Also, nice: learn a foreign language, an instrument, or immerse yourself in a new hobby. The greater your interest, the faster you will remember something.

12. More Tricks: Do you find it difficult to remember a phone number or a shopping list? Then make it a song. Music can aid memory so that something boring is better absorbed. Also, try to increase your concentration with the following exercise. For example, look at a plant, turn around, and draw as many details as possible. Then look again. Is the shape of the leaf, the pattern on the flower corrects? By looking more closely, you will learn to remember more details.

13. To Drink Water: Brains consist of more than seventy percent moisture. Those who drink too little will get a headache. That's because the brain has a lack of moisture. Drink two liters of water a day so that the moisture balance in the brain is maintained. It is the easiest way to keep the mind sharp.

14. Optimistic Thinking: Do you believe that your brain deteriorates rapidly as you get older? Research shows that older people score less well during memory tests if given damaging information about old age and memory beforehand. Persuade yourself that you have a great memory that will only get better.

Tricks to Improve Memory

If we don't have a lot of time to practice this type of game, there are several tricks that we can perform daily and almost automatically when we repeat them several times. They will help us improve our memory and concentrate better.

We will start by saying that sleeping well is a fundamental pillar to improve our memory, and we must do it between 7 and 9 hours a day. Our brain uses the hours of sleep to archive everything learned during the day and, if we do not give it the necessary time, it will not be able to save all the data correctly. If, also, we reinforce it with a nap, much better.

Opening and closing the hands are acts that help improve memory, according to a study from Montclair University, which revealed that clenching the right fist for 90 seconds helps in memory formation.

The meditation also reinforces memory. After two weeks of training, the University of California, Santa Barbara, confirms that improvements occur in reading comprehension and working memory and concentration.

For the University of Surrey, closing our eyes helps us remember more data (precisely 23% more) than if we open our eyes. If we accompany this action with a good coffee, as advocated by Johns Hopkins University, we will feel more active, and memory will be strengthened. But coffee should not be our only ally since chocolate also brings us great privileges. Some cocoa components, flavanols, contribute to better cognitive performance, stimulate neurogenesis, and cause learning area changes.

Although we are fully involved in training our minds, we must not neglect our bodies. We mostly know that exercising moderately helps you memorize what you have previously learned. This occurs thanks to the release of norepinephrine, induced by physical exercise, which allows us great benefits to remember information.

As we can see, there are several techniques and various tips to stimulate memory, and it is only up to us to choose the method that suits us best and to practice the different exercises regularly.

Habits to Prevent Memory Loss

Although it is true that with aging, this kind of cognitive ability deteriorates, we have a significant margin of maneuver to avoid, or at least delay, the appearance of confusion for a few years. Biology does not have to mark our lives totally: how we relate to our environment also counts.

Knowing the keys to not losing memory allows us to build a healthier brain with more significant mental agility by introducing a series of simple habits in our day to day.

Now, betting on integrating strategies into our lives to avoid losing memory means getting involved instantaneously. That is why it is worthy of knowing how to direct our efforts towards everything that is most effective.

Taking into account the above, you can follow these keys to protect your mental agility:

1. **Cultivate Your Social Life:** Relating to others often, be it with family and friends or participating in a group activity, promotes better memory, as various studies have shown. By interacting with other people, the brain neurons responsible for learning are stimulated, making them find new ways to connect.

2. **Personal Relationships Keep Neurons Active:** When there is a greater degree of interconnection between the networks of neurons that make the brain, it is easier to evoke memory through "alternative routes." That means that the possibilities of arriving at the same idea are multiplied, starting from sensations or thinking that has little to do with each other. In this way, even if there is an area of the brain that has been damaged, others can take over and lead our thinking to individual contents of memory.

3. **Change Your Routines:** Always doing the same thing leads the brain to adjust,

which favors premature aging. This happens because our brain gets used to working in a loop as it is always exposed to the same stimuli. Altering routines serves to prevent this kind of impoverishment of the mind because it makes our memories of past experiences richer and full of quick references. For example, you can try modifying the routes from home to work or to the areas you go to every day or changing the order of things you do at home as soon as you get up.

4. **Nourish Your Brain:** The brain is part of the organs that need the most energy, so it is good that you pay awareness to what you usually eat. If you do not eat correctly, the body will begin to "force" its operation to reach all its goals, leading to wear and tear that can affect you in the medium and long term. In this sense, all the studies point to the Mediterranean Diet as the ideal option; one of its secrets is the antioxidant power in the foods most used in it. Olive oil, fish (mostly blue), nuts, fruits and vegetables, and legumes or cereals should not be missing from your daily menus.

5. **Try Not to Stress:** High levels of stress trigger the amounts of cortisol, adrenaline, and norepinephrine that circulate through the body. Our body produces these substances, but according to various investigations, excessive amounts negatively affect memory, especially episodic memory (the one in charge of knowing when and where something has happened to us in the past). Anxiety makes it harder for the brain to generate new memories, as it focuses on short-term "here and now" stimuli to avoid possible imminent danger. Also, some studies indicate that chronic stress could even cause irreversible memory loss. Excess Hormones Linked to Stress, Such as Cortisol, Impair Memory: The massages, relaxation techniques, and even diet changes (food and relaxing plants) can help you reduce your anxiety levels.

6. **Boost Cardiovascular Exercise:** Physical activity helps protect the brain from premature cognitive decline and reduces neurodegenerative disease risk. Exercise increases the brain's oxygenation and, in turn, increased blood flow in this organ

appears to reduce the levels of a protein (TAU) closely linked to Alzheimer's.

7. **Avoid Being Overweight**: Research from Boston University (USA) maintains a direct relationship between excess fat in the body and a smaller brain volume.

8. **Accumulated Fat Has a Direct Effect on The Brain:** Besides, it seems that abdominal fat would be especially harmful since it increases the risk of dementia over the years. In this case, the calories we consume also count: eating more than we need produces oxidative damage that can cause structural changes in the brain.

9. **Sleep Well:** After a "bad night," you will have found that it is more difficult for you to retain any simple data the next day. This is normal, as getting a good night's sleep promotes concentration and attention. According to a study by the Scripps Research Institute (USA) published in the journal "Cell," during sleep, the brain slows down the activity of a type of neurons associated with forgetting, which helps retain memories better.

10. **Challenge Your Mind:** Doing accounts "upside-down," crosswords or puzzles, learning a language, adapting to the use of new technology, or only going to an exhibition or show ... these are exercises that stimulate the brain and help it maintain its agility. This is one of the most useful measures to avoid losing memory.

11. **Avoid Toxins That "Steal" Your Memory:** Tobacco, alcohol, and excessively fatty foods are detrimental to proper brain function. Taking prodrugs for a long time can also impair memory and daily contact with solvents, paints, or glues.

12. **Thrill:** Numerous experiments have shown that memories associated with an intense emotional charge achieve better memory consolidation.

Foods That Help Memory and Intelligence

The food you eat alters the performance of your brain. "Eat right to increase your IQ, improve your mood, sharpen your memory, and keep your mind active." Good powers of concentration depend on keeping messages flowing freely between brain cells. These cells need oxygen to turn on and send a message, and they get it from blood sugar.

Simply ensuring an adequate and consistent caloric intake throughout the day is the first step in staying focused and alert. However, it is not enough for the signals to be generated; they must also be sent from one cell to another. Nerve fibers do this. Like electrical cables, these fibers must be insulated for messages to flow. To build these sheaths, the brain needs a fatty substance called myelin.

Omega-3 oils (found mainly in oily fish and walnuts, pumpkin seeds, and flax seeds) help build and maintain myelin. This may be why fish oil supplements seem to boost children's mental performance, although studies showing this are controversial.

Our ability to remember things depends on brain cells making new connections. They do best when they are very excited, which is why we tend to reflect on events that occur when we are emotionally or intellectually stimulated.

When you are anxious, your body produces stress hormones called glucocorticoids. These trigger the brain to search for ways to alleviate misery. And that's where sugary and fatty foods

come in. Foods rich in iron are very beneficial for maintaining healthy brain cells.

To work as well as possible, your brain cells need an adequate supply of oxygen. Lack of iron in your diet can lessen your blood's ability to carry oxygen, reducing the amount transported to your brain. Not getting sufficient iron can also cause problems like poor concentration, low strength, and tiredness.

Lean red meat is an outstanding origin of iron. Excellent vegetarian iron sources include egg yolks, legumes like kidney beans and lentils, dried apricots, fortified breakfast cereals, broccoli, whole grains, and whole wheat bread.

If hundreds of notes cover your desk and your cell phone is full of reminders, maybe it is time for you to make changes to your daily diet. Although we generally blame age for forgetfulness, this ability can be significantly improved with proper nutrition.

"Having a good memory depends on your total brain cells, the connection between them, and your health," says Joy Bauer.

The expert suggests that you eat these foods that will help you avoid memory loss:

1. Beets to Regulate the Heart Rate

A good heartbeat means a healthy brain. "Every cell in the body needs an uninterrupted supply of oxygen and nutrients to stay alive and function properly," says Bauer. Maintaining the correct pressure levels (less than 120/80), exercising regularly, and consuming foods such as beets help improve blood circulation, ensuring the brain's supply of nutrients. "A brain full of well-nourished neurons allows you to think and remember more clearly," says Bauer.

2. Fish to Keep Brain Cells Healthy

"As regards to food and memory, fish can be the star," says Bauer. Fish such as salmon, sardines, and herring contain reasonable amounts of omega-3s essential for maintaining healthy brain cells. Bauer recommends eating some of these fish at least three times a week.

3. Wild Fruits to Prevent Neuron Failure

Berries are high in antioxidants that help prevent the breakdown of brain cells. A Harvard study found that women who eat at least one cup of blackberries and strawberries a week experience a 2.5-year delay in mental decline compared to women who did not consume them. "Specifically, blueberries have attracted attention because they facilitate memory and learning," says Bauer. The expert recommends eating four cups of blackberries a week. Although it is not in season, frozen ones are also nutritious.

4. Fat-Free Protein to Improve Cognitive Abilities

Chicken and turkey breast, eggs, and low-fat milk are excellent sources of vitamin B12, which is an essential protein for maintaining cognitive skills. A 2012 study by Tufts University showed that older adults who were low in vitamin B12 were at higher risk for mental decline.

5. Walnuts to Boost Memory

Walnuts might look like a miniature type of the human brain for a reason. A study published in the Journal of Alzheimer's Disease found that consuming walnuts was linked to better memory scores and cognitive functions.

6. Coffee to Improve Focus

Caffeine can temporarily enhance Focus and memory. Although Bauer says that a couple of coffee cups a day is fine, she recommends avoiding caffeine eight hours before bed to interfere with sleep.

7. Spinach, Broccoli, and Other Green Leafy Vegetables

Several studies suggest that spinach and broccoli can help protect against age-related problems and cognitive deficits. Both vegetables are rich in iron, an essential mineral that helps transport oxygen throughout the body.

8. Eggs

Free-range eggs are packed with brain-protecting omega-3 fatty acids. Eggs have even been called the perfect food for the brain. But not all eggs are created equal.

Eggs from free-range chickens, raised outside on green grass pastures, contain twice as much omega-3 as standard store-bought eggs and three times as much natural vitamin E, a potent antidepressant and possible antidote to Alzheimer's disease.

Make sure to eat the yolks - free-range eggs are rich in choline, a brain-stimulating compound that promotes neurotransmitter health.

9. Beans

Beans are often failed to observe, but they are a great inexpensive ingredient to add to your shopping list. They contain an ideal mix of complex carbohydrates and proteins; This permits them to be digested slowly, which ultimately helps stabilize glucose levels and curb fatigue.

10. Dark Chocolate

According to some studies at Harvard University, chocolate can increase the brain's blood supply, giving it more fuel for the work it does. The most advisable thing is not to outreach its consumption.

11. Apples

"An apple a day keeps the doctor away" is very likely when you consider that this formidable fruit contains catechin. These substances show promise to protect us from brain-damaging chemicals prevalent in everyday products. Just be sure to choose organic apples; catechins are in the fruit's skin, the part exposed to pesticides in chemical agriculture.

12. Cayenne Pepper

Hot peppers are rich in capsaicin, a pain reliever and fat fighter that research suggests may help you cut calories and aid in the body's fat breakdown. When next you're preparing a meal, instead of having the salt or black pepper, the smartest option maybe a pinch of cayenne.

13. The Avocados

Avocados offer so much more than just a creamy, delicious flavor. They also give your brain a boost - research shows, for example, that their high levels of monounsaturated fatty acids can help keep nerve cells in the brain healthy.

Each avocado serving has 20 different vitamins, including potassium, which studies suggest can help control blood pressure and lutein, helping protect your eyes.

The Power of the Mind

The human mind is powerful; it allows people to live a perfect everyday life with only 20% brains. The chronicles of the world are the history of some men who believed in themselves. That one belief, which self-confidence brought out the very best in them. You can do anything, achieve anything. You only fail if you don't strive to develop the power of self-confidence in yourself. Once someone or a nation loses confidence in itself, death inevitably follows.

Self-confidence, independence from others, independence self-confidence, self-confidence, and self-confidence are the secret to greatness. If you believe in all three hundred and thirty million things, and you still don't believe in yourself, then there's no hope for you; you will never achieve anything.

Never think that something is unfeasible for you. It is the greatest sin to think like that. If there is sin, the only evil is to believe that I am weak and cannot achieve anything myself. What you think you are going to be. When you look back into your past, you will find that you kept trying to get help from others, but it never came. All the support that came from yourself, from within.

Successful people create their reality wisely, using the brain's power to make the outcomes they want in life. They genuinely trust they can accomplish whatever they put their mind to.

Disregarding their existing circumstances, they have faith in themselves. They talk only about what they want in life, feed their minds with positive news, and be surrounded by inspirational people, thereby attracting memorable experiences.

Contrarily, the rest of society imprisons them, creating four walls around them. Every thought makes misery, repeatedly playing sad stories, reciting the same script like a record continuously playing time after time. Stories that tell the world of their scarcity thinking, complaining, and choosing to blame others for their general lack in life.

The power of the mind is done in two directions.

The mind's power does not doubt that "mentalization" / "suggestion" has a significant influence on health. This principle works in two directions: peoplē who show a high degree of faith, self-confidence, who have the habit of meditating, praying, visualize or make some mental projection, respond better to treatments and become ill. However, the opposite occurs in people subjected to chronic stress, with low self-confidence, pessimists, and who, in short, do not use their mind to help their body. These people are more likely to get sick, respond worse to treatment, and have poorer health. Thus, all of them contribute to developing self-control mechanisms.

Facts That Help You Unleash the Power of Your Mind

For every thought you have, an outpour of electrical currents from your brain releases an unspecified number of neurochemicals in charge of the operation of your nervous system. Your body acknowledges each thought accordingly, like a world-class conductor guiding a famous orchestra, with everything working in unity from your heart, liver, and lungs carrying out their role with accuracy.

What, where, how, and the time allotment we give awareness to something in life, alongside our monotonous thoughts, forms our neurological wiring.

Concentrating on the pain that exists within your body transmits electrical currents to your mind that continually releasing the pain.

Uninteresting thoughts create connections in the brain that quickly become ironclad. These thoughts move from conscious to unconscious methods of thinking and being. That is how we behave on auto-pilot.

The action of change needs falling to remember what we know to uncover new ways of being. Continuous meditation practices accelerate the achievement of this goal and give exact positive results.

Gaining something new requires considerable energy and our undivided attention. Consider when you first practiced driving a car the level of engagement you possessed compared to an experienced driver operating on auto-pilot. We can alter who we are with every new piece of information that we learn. By combining this further information with practical application, a unique occurrence is brought to life. We call on more significant

volumes of change; the more we continue with this process.

Our life-long repetitive negative thoughts are notable contributors to stress and disease in the body. Stress causes us to live in a 'survival' state, which negatively changes our internal state and exhausts our body—in turn, giving unfavorable responses, which include anger, depression, misery, or confusion. When we are here in this state, it can be compared to acting like a bird caught in a cage or a prisoner held in prison; we fail to see our lives' possibilities. This is why people become 'stuck' for their persistent emotional state is the highly addictive resultant of the production of neurochemicals.

There are four central areas in the brain. The frontal lobe is near all the plastic parts of the brain in charge of decision-making. The cerebral cortex or neocortex is for our 'free will.' It stores 90% of our brain's neurons and manages information, attention, awareness, thoughts, language, and recordings of our knowledge and experiences. The parietal lobe processes sensory communication, with the temporal lobe taking control of smell, sounds, speech, and vision.

Our genes affect our behavior, yet research demonstrates that we can produce positive changes. In 1942, Conrad Waddington introduced the term 'Epigenetics,' which affects genetics on development. Those successful in making change studied others via education, utilizing books, movies, and inspirational people to expand new thoughts and create new ways of being. Visualization is a powerful tool used to

energize the brain to generate strong mind-body connections.

Our state of being consists of the repetitive cycle of our constant thoughts joined with the manufacturing of chemicals within our body, which generates our emotions. This repetitive cycle has an impact on our behavior.

To make a change in reality and heal our bodies, the secret ingredient lies in making up our minds to do so. We can fully recover and change our external situations just like those patients who are told they could never walk again yet do such, sports stars that suffer from irreversible injuries, however fully recover, or those who have suffered life-threatening cancer and a few months later it is nowhere to be found. They know the secret has a powerful purpose, believing they have the power to change their circumstances, determination, and the will to create what they want in life.

There is a relationship between acquiring knowledge and life experiences. Our mind is provided with knowledge via the brain, while our mind elicits our experiences through our body.

The Power of the Mind upon the Body

This perspective will give us enormous self-esteem; it will start us to have "faith in ourselves. "In the words of Albert Einstein, "the mind is like the parachute ... it only works if we have it open. "The key is to master your thoughts. Let's see, reflect: do you let your brain and your thoughts rule you? Or do you rather use the power of the mind to dominate your thoughts? It would be best if you always remembered that "the manifestations of the body accompany the thought." You know, you decide because this is precisely one of the aspects that make the difference between mental health and illness. Descartes' famous quotation is worth it here: «I think; therefore, I am.» The truth is that we can do everything our mind can imagine since we only use 1% of our mental capacity. Some people learn to optimize their minds to the maximum.

A reasonable observer will know that a sick person can recover more quickly if he has positive thinking. In contrast, someone who is dominated by negative thoughts takes much longer to recover and, in some cases, their weakness or condition worsens. As Bob Marley said: "No one but one can free his mind from slavery."

Mind's Power

Who knows the power of the mind?
I have repeatedly asked myself this question; perhaps my subconscious does not allow me to assimilate how powerful it is when acting and carrying out all its tasks.
Lately, I have experienced what we call pressure; I think this is the only state in which a person shows himself as he is; It is strange how you manage to keep feelings, problems, and thoughts in yourself; the accumulation of these is what leads you to explode and say "I'm tired, I can't go on with this."
Sometimes we call pressure to fear to keep fighting; powerlessness may be part of it.
Feeling that you can do a lot, but you can't do anything; Terrible feeling, no? Whenever impotence takes hold of you, relax, meditate, and then act smartly, you may do more than expected.

It is the mind that generates millions of emotions, thoughts, and even obstacles in your life, many times; we think about carrying out an idea, and we do nothing because a thorn crosses our mind. "The excuse," you see, this one also knows how to play in our against; do not pay attention or create vague excuses that can obstruct your way to success, as long as you do the right thing and are clear about what you are looking for and want follow your instincts, maybe things will not turn out as bad as you expect.

I think that our mind is a powerful source capable of creating artificial clouds hiding all reality; sometimes, it is only a strategy to avoid all pain and suffering; Most times, the human being uses them as a pretext for not seeing what is in front of his eyes.

I want to get to with this because our mind has many methods: defense, obstruction, or only evasion; the important thing about this is to learn to handle it; acting with intelligence and sanity, you will know what to do.

Who says you can't? Your mind is capable of rendering you useless to the point of making you believe that you are worthless.

Let your security and self-esteem is an impulse to believe that everything is possible, thus avoiding any mental obstacle.

Nothing is impossible; there are single things that require more effort and dedication.

You will see for yourself if you focus a positive thought on an area of your body where you feel discomfort. You have to convince yourself of the power of your mind to promote healing. I advise you to put it into practice for yourself and start to experience it. As my dear colleague, Christiaan Barnard used to say, "It's all in your attitude of mind."

I suggest you make an effort: immediately erase from your mind any negative thoughts that come up, the ones that generate doubt, fear, guilt, and regrets. Recreate your mind with positive reviews that create feelings of well-being, confidence, understanding, and curiosity. In this sense, one of my favorite books is The Secret of Rhonda Byrne, which teaches you many of these keys. "When you emit the perfect frequency of what you want, the law of attraction will force all people, circumstances, and events to receive it". Think positive.

10 Keys to Developing Mental Power

1. Know What the Mind Is Made Of
Everyone thinks that the reason is that the head, the brain, what we believe with ... But no, the mind is more. The rational part is just a small portion. In humans, three brains coexist:
The reptilian brain, which is the most primitive and instinctive part houses the species' survival mechanisms.
The limbic brain, in which emotions develop.
And the neocortex brain, which houses thought processes, is divided into two: the left hemisphere (analytical, rational part) and the right hemisphere (creative, intuitive part).
Which one predominates? The rational part, of course, we are homo sapiens; we came out of the caves! ... Well no. The reptilian brain predominates and also in everything. Perhaps one of the fields in which this is best verified is in the purchasing process.

2.Watch Your Thinking
It all starts with a thought and you are free to choose.
If you know your thought processes, you will notice the mental chatter we talked about earlier. Perceiving it and selecting what you want to inhabit your mind gives you the freedom to

shape it however you want, and a clean sense is a healthy and productive mind. Discover, therefore, who is taking steps in your mind and stop him.

3.Divergent Thinking

We have already discussed lateral thinking and divergent thinking before. It is merely a matter of using the mind differently than usual, finding solutions outside the known channels to access quantum fields in which everything can be created.

This, which sounds very bombastic, translates into things like:

Embrace disruption (possibility of sudden changes, outside of logic and geometric progression).

Challenge evidence and assumptions.

Practice free association of ideas.

4. Silent Knowledge

There is a type of knowledge called silent knowledge. The first time I read about him was in the work of Carlos Castaneda.

It is the knowledge that flows fluidly and without words from within each being. When it comes to me, I know it's him because I can't find words to describe him. The known human language is insufficient for me to express a block of knowledge that, in itself, springs from me, emerges from the interior of my being, and forms a set of information that cannot be translated into words.

You can seek it out and bring it up, of course, but not force it. One of my favorite techniques is to adopt a contemplative and meditative state, in which I rest and remain silent without seeking but being receptive to whatever arises. What emerges is not an alien or spirit voice. It is merely your voice, the voice of yourself in a higher version (your higher self).

In other words: you access your quantum self in which you exist at different levels or vibrations and connect with the higher one, the one who has the information.

5.Food

As we have already risen to the celestial spheres, we will descend a little bit not to forget contact with reality.

We are people, and we need to eat. Depending on what you eat, you can either help your mind or harm it. Here are a few foods that I gorge on that are very beneficial for mental processes: blueberries, avocado, walnuts, and salmon.

6.Full Awareness

Everyone's consciousness can be scattered or focused on things other than what we are doing. When we practice full Focus (anchoring in the present moment), we access a more profound level where the mind is centered and free from thought. At this level, there is no dispersion, and we favor the appearance of responses.

7.Breathing

And it is not worth saying I already do it! I know, I suppose, but it is good to do it calmly, ritually, and with the awareness that you are oxygenating the brain, feeding it. When you walk, you can take advantage of watching television when you do meditation, cross stitch... and breathe consciously.

8.Act as If

This technique is potent and is recommended in countless places. I first read it in Conversations with God by Donald Walsch, but afterward, it has continued to come from multiple locations.

It consists of acting as if you already have what you want to have or have already achieved what you want to achieve.

Imagine that a mind is a wish-granting machine (which it is). You cannot ask with the conscience of getting something that you do not have or something that you lack; that is a great mistake.

9.New Habits

To develop the power of the mind, we have to open different ways in it than usual.

Our way of thinking, being, doing fixes in the brain paths (neural connections) makes us obtain the same type of results in the same kind of circumstances.

To get out of that circle, you have to create a new neural connection, which are achieved by doing different things and leaving the comfort zone. Taking further actions or adopting new habits, the more distant from the previous ones, the better, create new possibilities in the brain through neurons' associations.

10. Sixth sense

Sometimes I see dead ...

No, I don't mean that sixth sense.

I mean intuition as a form of intelligence.

Indeed, because intuition, far from being discarded, represents a way of communicating and knowing. Specifically, it can mean them direct perception of the truth, of a fact, independently of any reasoning process.

Therefore, we discuss developing the inner voice and understanding that it is a superior version of mental development: the one that takes you directly to the truth without going through any road but by teleporting you.

DEFINITION OF THE SUBCONSCIOUS

The subconscious is simply a part of our mind that we do not see. For practical purposes, we have a kind of veil that prevents us from seeing a part of our reason.

However, this veil does not modify the mind's structure; it merely makes a part of it hidden. It's like putting a curtain that separates a room in two. The curtain does not change the room's size or its content; it merely makes it impossible to see the other from one side. Well, the veil that divides our mind does something similar: it does not modify our mind; it hides merely a part.

This veil is not a very strong parting. It is not a stone wall; it is merely a curtain. If we do nothing, it prevents us from seeing what is on the other side, but it is relatively easy to remove it. This means that we can all access our subconscious if we want to. We have to make an effort to achieve it; we do not have access to it automatically.

But what kind of information do we store in the subconscious?

The information that we have stored there and to which we cannot easily access consciousness usually contains deep fears, repressed desires, and traumatic experiences that even consciously we would not like to remember. All this content can lead to the appearance of specific pathologies such as certain anxiety disorders, fears, phobias, etc.

However, despite how difficult it is for us to access the subconscious, all those contents that we have stored there, we usually unconsciously express them in different ways.

Examples of expression of the subconscious

- **Dreams:** a person who suffered a traumatic childhood experience may have plans related to it even if they do not even consciously remember it.

- **Unconscious actions:** a person who coldly represses his homosexuality becomes uninhibited and approaches people of the same sex when he consumes alcohol.

- **The lapsus linguae:** when we talk about a topic, we suddenly say a word or phrase not related to it.

The moments in which this type of information that we have stored in the subconscious usually comes to light occur when our consciousness level decreases.

Why Do We Have A Subconscious?

This transformation that causes a part of our mind to be blocked at birth is part of the human being's design. In other words, it is not a mistake or a coincidence; it is a planned phenomenon.

Also, we are responsible for this design. No one has imposed it on us, but we created the Earth freely, and we decided that everyone who came here should leave behind a part of the contents of their mind.

The big question is: why? Why did we decide to hide a part of our mind? Well, to be able to do what we wanted to do. The qualities of the human body and mind are perfectly designed for a particular objective. And this objective is none other than enhancing our creativity.

Have you ever thought about starting life over? In some cases, it might be okay, right? Leaving behind everything you have experienced and starting from scratch. It would also imply some difficulties because you would lose everything you learned with experience, but, on the other hand, you would gain a lot of freshness and spontaneity. You would be like a child again.

Earth exists to offer this possibility to anyone who wants it. It is a planet designed explicitly so that any "soul" who wishes can experience for a time what it is like to start a life from scratch.

And to create a life from scratch, we must forget the past.

The subconscious is the place where we leave our past when we come to Earth. It's a bit like a "wardrobe" where we keep everything we don't need to go here. And when we leave the planet, we get everything back.

How Does the Subconscious Work?

Our subconscious functions as a kind of emitter of messages or stimuli that we process at a conscious level and activate specific behavior patterns without being aware of it. In other words, the decisions we make every day, even if it seems that we are making them consciously, are highly influenced by our subconscious.

Our subconscious is as if it were a computer program that we have been creating over the years with the experiences we have been storing.

This same program (composed of ideas, ingrained beliefs, thoughts, etc.) causes us to lean more towards a decision than another.

Sometimes our subconscious mind is following our true desires. We make the decisions that we want; however, in others, it is not, and there is so much negative information that we have stored and accumulated over the years from childhood, we can become self-sabotaging.

Various researchers have determined that our subconscious is a source of creativity and that it helps us solve problems, even those that seem to have no solution. This has been demonstrated through various studies, one of which is quite interesting shows how we become more creative using our subconscious mind.

Ways to Grow the Vast Power of Your Subconscious

The subconscious is a storage space with unlimited capacity; all your memories, past experiences, deepest beliefs, everything you have experienced is stored permanently. The subconscious is a part of you outside of your consciousness, which creates automatic programs to make life easier without paying attention to everything you do.

The iceberg's exact part for the conscious mind and the submerged part speak to our unconscious.

It resembles driving a vehicle; a youthful driver who is figuring out how to go will be focused on driving without engaging in conversation. But with time and practice, this person will feel comfortable driving, which will become a registered habit in the subconscious.

The subconscious doesn't stop being active, all day and all night, whether you do something or not. It also monitors your body's functions, such as breathing, heart rate, and even the nervous system.

Your subconscious takes control of your life 95% of the time. On the contrary, during the first six years of your life, your subconscious is

programmed and very powerful compared to your conscious mind.

The goal of the subconscious is to make sure you respond precisely the way you were programmed. Your subconscious records everything you say and adjusts it to a pattern consistent with your self-concept, your "Main program." That is the reason it is so crucial to filter what happens in your subconscious.

But how can you adjust it to make significant changes in your life? Your thoughts have the power to overt into reality. The choices belong to you.

1.The Power of Positive Affirmations:

To change your life, you don't just have to change your mind; you need to go further and change your schedule. It takes time to program your subconscious with the current "conscious" understanding you have gained because you have to destroy old neural pathways and develop new connections in your brain.

But what is right is that the subconscious learns through repetition; this is how it disclosed negative ways or bad habits. By affirming your new beliefs/programs or thinking method every day, you can truly change your life and reality.

Each day, take the time to sow the seeds of your new programming. Repetition of positive affirmations has the strength to upraise your vibrations and print in your subconscious.

According to Paramahansa Yogananda, "Loud or silent repetition of inspirational words has proven effective in various psychotherapy systems; the secret lies in the increase of the vibrational frequency of the mind."

Statements to be considered:

"I love myself and respect myself."

"I am full of peace, harmony, and joy."

"I bring good things into my life."

"My positive thoughts lead to positive things."

It's not just about repeatedly repeating the same thing; you have to break the obstacle that prevents specific thoughts from entering your subconscious. If you continuously feed your brain positive reviews, they will, in the end, enter your subconscious.

Grant only what you want and not what you don't want. At that time, if you have negative thoughts, sadness, anxiety, frustration, etc., don't try to resist these thoughts, but acknowledge and accept them in your conscious mind.

2. Meditate.

Meditation takes you into deeper realms of consciousness, allowing you to access your subconscious. In our waking consciousness, our brain functions on a "beta" model.

This state is connected to alertness but also stress, anger, and anxiety. During meditation, your brain patterns slow down and go first into

Alpha, then into Theta, and a triangle in deep meditation.

It will get more comfortable; you will become the observer of your thoughts instead of being distracted. Let your ideas circulate, and don't react. It is at this time that you will begin to access your subconscious through meditation.

3. Be Creative.

Unleash your creativity by artistically expressing yourself, for example, with painting, drawing, cooking, decorating, sculpture, ceramics, etc. By encouraging your imagination, you can get closer to your subconscious.

4. Follow Your Intuition.

"Your vision becomes clearer when you can look into your heart. Whoever looks outside himself is only dreaming; he who looks within wakes up."- CG Jung.

Intuition is what associates the subconscious and the conscious mind. Your subconscious is continuously communicating with the conscious. It is the internal voice or "intuition" that you need to hear.

There are other various ways to unleash the power of your subconscious mind, such as clinical hypnotherapy, energy psychology, and even brainwave entertainment. When you start living in harmony with your inner self and subconscious state, you will transform your life.

How to Use the Secrets of Your Subconscious?

Like it or not, your subconscious commands you. It has immense power in controlling your life experiences: from how you react to situations to the actions you do every day, how much you earn, and even the type of food you eat.

Your subconscious beliefs guide your every action. Even when you make a conscious determination to go after something you want, it is your subconscious that determines what you will do and how you will do it; it is your "autopilot." It is pre-programmed to follow a specific route, and it is not possible to deviate from that route unless you change the programmed directions first.

Here are five ways you can use the secrets of your subconscious. They are different from each other, but they can also be complementary;

choose what best suits your needs and preferences. Proceed consistently and with awareness. The results will be seen soon, and your reality will change forever.

1.ENVIRONMENTAL INFLUENCES

Have you ever thought of the effect of your environment on your subconscious? Remember that your subconscious is constantly absorbing information, concluding, and setting up beliefs based on that information. If your daily environment is full of negativity and conflict, imagine what types of messages are being soaked up into your mind. Your kick-off is to strictly limit the negativity you are exposed to from this point on. Avoid reading negative news and avoid spending too much time with people we could define as "toxic" or negative. Instead, look for positive information to read and absorb and spend most of your time with positive, successful people. Over time you will find that more encouraging messages are absorbed into your mind.

2. DISPLAY

Your subconscious responds well to images. The inward eye is a perfect way to program your mind with positive and powerful images. Try to spend 10-15 minutes a day visualizing festive scenes about you and your life occurrences. Here are not many things you may need to imagine: Plenty of money, a lovely home, satisfying relationships, an exciting job, health, and a slim, fit body.

When you do this consistently, you end up redrawing the negative images stored by your past experiences, fears, worries, and doubts. To further increase the power of visualization, be sure to accompany the visualization with healthy and positive emotions. As you imagine these beautiful things in your mind, you feel the emotions attached to them. Allow the feelings of love, joy, gratitude, and peace to flow through you as if you were genuinely experiencing these experiences. Your subconscious will absorb the messages as if they were real!

This is the true beauty of visualization: the power to ignore limiting messages and focus on pleasing images, which are absorbed directly into your subconscious to be reproduced later.

3. STATEMENTS

Affirmations are another successful way to install positive messages in your subconscious.

They work best if you observe a few simple rules:

Express them positively in the present tense. Tell yourself phrases like "I am confident and successful" and not "I will be confident and successful"; this is because your subconscious only knows the present moment. Also, use positive affirmations. Saying "I am not a failure" is absorbed as "I am a failure" since your subconscious cannot process the negative concepts.

Recall the corresponding feelings. Saying, "I'm rich" while feeling poor only sends conflicting messages to your subconscious! Whatever you are saying at the moment, try to feel the corresponding emotions because your subconscious will be more likely to believe it.

Repeat; affirmations don't work if you say them once or twice. Repeat these several times throughout the day for the best results. The fantastic thing about this process is that you can fit it perfectly into your routine.

4.BINAURAL SOUNDS AND BRAIN ENTRAINMENT

Another standard method is the use of audio recordings that intentionally alter the frequency of your brain waves. It may feel like something out of a sci-fi movie, but reports from people who have tried these audios are incredibly positive. Your brain waves vibrate at specific frequency levels, depending on what you are doing at any given time: Gamma when you are occupied in certain motor functions, Beta when you are fully conscious and actively concentrating, Alpha when you are relaxed, Theta when you are sleepy or slightly asleep, Delta when in a deep sleep. Binaural sounds occur when two tones are played at different frequencies, triggering the brain waves to follow a different pattern. For instance, if you want to move from stress to relaxation, listen to an audio that activates the alpha state. This audio programming can help you reprogram your subconscious by creating a more receptive state for installing positive messages. Research has shown that your subconscious is more receptive to new information when you are very relaxed, such as in alpha or theta states.

5. HYPNOSIS

Hypnosis can be just as effective as Brain Entrainment audio programming, except it doesn't use frequencies that alter brain waves.
The hypnotist gradually talks to you in a more relaxed and receptive state and delivers positive

and constructive messages to your subconscious. There is also a more "intimate" version, so to speak, of hypnosis: self-hypnosis.

This is a smart option, where you use pre-recorded audio instead of living hypnosis sessions. You can even make a record of your voice if you think someone else's is distracting you; in this way, you will be able to hear your voice repeat affirmations or suggestions as if you were telling them yourself.

It is essential to give this reprogramming process time to work. Don't expect to see immediate changes.

Be confident and steadfast in using these and all other methods available to reprogram the subconscious. As soon as these transformations become evident, you will feel motivated to progress, but you persist until that happens.

And know that these changes are lasting and powerful.

How to Grow Your Brain Power at Any Age?

A good memory depends on the health and health of your brain. Whether you are a student reading for the final exam or an expert interested in doing something to pay attention to mentally, your problem gray as you get older. Even if you are a senior who wants to take care of and improve, there is a lot to do. You can do to boost your memory and mental performance.

They say you can't teach old dogs new tricks, but scientists realize this old saying isn't true when it comes to brains. The human brain has an exceptional ability to adapt and change with old age. This ability is known as neuroplasticity. With the right stimuli, the brain can form new neural pathways, alter existing relationships, adapt and respond in ever-changing ways.

The brain's extraordinary ability to transform occurs between learning and memory. You can use the natural power of neuroplastic to improve your cognitive skills, your ability to learn new information, and your memory of all ages.

These nine tips show you how.

Tip 1: Train Your Brain

In adulthood, the brain develops millions of neural pathways, processes; stores information quickly, solves family problems, and performs everyday activities with minimal mental effort. I will do it. But if you are always on this path, you are not giving the stimulus your brain needs to keep growing and developing. You have to change the situation from time to time!

Memory, like muscle strength, needs to "use it or lose it." The more you coach your brain, the better information processing and memory will be. However, not all activities are created equal.

The best brain training breaks your routine and challenges you to develop using new brain pathways.

The four keys to good brain development activity

- **It teaches you something new**.

No matter how demanding an intellectual activity is, it is not a good exercise for your brain if you are already proficient. These types of activities are not unfamiliar to you and should be outside of your comfort zone. To strengthen the brain, you must learn and continue to develop new skills.

- **This is compelling:** The best brain training activities require your full and in-depth attention. It is not enough that the action is beneficial. It still requires spiritual effort. For example, it is vital to learn how to play interesting new songs. I'm not playing hard songs that you remember already.
- **These are skills you can develop:** Start at a reasonable level and look for activities that increase as your skills improve and always increase your limits and improve your skills. When the previous story is hard to get comfortable with, it's time to work on the next performance level.
- **This is useful:** Awards support the brain learning process. The more interested and occupied you are in your business, the more likely you will follow it and the more profits you will make. So, choose activities that are beneficial but still fun and rewarding.

Summary for men playing acoustic guitar Think of the new things you always want to try, such as playing the guitar, making pottery, making a donut, playing chess, speaking French, dancing the tango, and learning. All these activities help improve memory while maintaining arousal and participation.

What about brain-training programs?
Many brain training apps and online programs promise to improve memory, problem-solving skills, attention, and even IQ through daily training. But do they work? More and more evidence say no. This brain training program can provide short-term improvements in the specific tasks or games you practice. Still, it seems to improve or improve your general intelligence, memory, or cognitive skills. No.

Tip 2: Don't Stop Exercising
Mental training is vital for brain health, but that doesn't mean you can't sweat. Exercise helps your brain stay awake. This increases oxygen to the brain and reduces the risk of memory loss-causing disorders, such as diabetes and cardiovascular disease. Exercise also increases the effectiveness of beneficial brain chemicals and reduces stress hormones. Perhaps more importantly, exercise plays an essential role in neuroplasty by boosting growth factors and stimulating new neuronal relationships.

Exercise tips that stimulate the brain

Aerobic exercise is excellent for your brain, so choose activities that keep your blood flowing. Generally, everything that is good for your heart is right for your brain.

When I wake up, is it a long time before I get rid of the sleep fog? If so, you may find that working out in the morning before you start your day makes a huge difference. In addition to cleaning spider webs, it prepares you to work all day.

Physical activity that requires hand-eye coordination or complex motor skills is beneficial in building the brain.

Exercise rest can help you cope with mental fatigue and evening depression. Even a short walk or a few jumps can be enough to reboot the brain.

Tip 3: Get Sleep
There is a massive distinction between the amount of sleep you get and the amount you need to study as well as you can. The truth is that more than 95% of adults need 7.5 to 9 hours of sleep each night to avoid sleep deprivation. Just a few hours will make the difference! Memory, creativity, problem solving, and critical thinking are entirely impaired.

However, sleep is more fundamental and essential for learning and memory. Research shows that memory integration requires sleep and important memory enhancement activities occur at deeper sleep levels.

Follow your regular sleep schedule. I sleep at the same time every night and wake up at the same time every morning. Do not disrupt your routine, even on weekends and holidays.

Keep away from all screens at least an hour before bedtime. The blue light emitted by televisions, tablets, phones, and computers cause arousal and suppress hormones such as melatonin, making you sleepy.

Cut down on caffeine. Caffeine has different effects on humans. Some people are susceptible, and even coffee in the morning can interfere with sleep at night. If it seems to warn you, try to reduce or eliminate it.

Tip 4: Make Time for Your Friends
When thinking about improving memory, think of "serious" activities like tackling New York Times puzzles, and mastering chess strategy. Alternatively, you can have even more fun, e.g., play with friends or enjoy fun movies, understanding? If you're like most of us, it's likely old. However, countless studies have shown that a fun life with friends brings cognitive benefits.

Healthy Relationship: Ultimate Brain Enhancer

Humans are very social animals. We don't want to survive alone.

Relationships stimulate our brain: in fact, interactions with others can allow the brain to move at its best.

Studies show that meaningful friendships and a healthy support system are essential not only for emotional health but also for brain health. For example, in a recent study at the Harvard School of Public Health, researchers initiated that people with the most agile social lives had the least memory loss.

There are many ways that you can take advantage of the brain and memory enhancement benefits of socialization. Volunteer, join clubs, meet friends more often, and contact them by phone. If you don't have a person, don't miss out on pets' value, especially sociable dogs.

Tip 5: Control Stress

Stress is one of the brain's enemies. After a while, chronic stress destroys brain cells and damages the hippocampus, areas of the brain involved in creating new and old memories. Studies have also linked stress to amnesia.

Tips for dealing with stress

- Set realistic expectations (and you can say no!)
- Take a break all-day.
- Express instead of inflating emotions
- Find a healthy equilibrium between work and leisure.
- Focus on one activity at a time, not multitasking

Benefits of Meditation to Relieve Stress and Improve Memory

Scientific evidence of the psychological benefits of meditation continues to mount. Studies have made known that meditation can help improve various conditions, including depression, anxiety, chronic pain, diabetes, and high blood pressure. Meditation can also improve concentration, creativity, memory, learning, and thinking.

Meditation does its "magic" by changing the real brain. Images of the brain show that regular meditators do more in the left prefrontal cortex, an area of the brain related to feelings of joy and calm. Meditation also increases the cerebral cortex's thickness and promotes more connections between brain cells, which increase mental acuity and memory performance.

Tip 6: Laugh

You more likely than not heard that laughing is the best medication, but it applies to the body, brain, and memory. Unlike emotional responses, which are limited to some brain regions, laughter takes up more areas of the entire brain.

Also, hearing jokes and studying jokes stimulate the brain's essential areas for learning and creativity. As the psychologist, Daniel Goleman points out in his book "Emotional Intelligence," that "laughing helps people think broader and behave more freely."

Are you looking for a technique to bring more laughter into your life? Let's start with these basics.

Please laugh for you. Share your bad moments. The best way to take yourself too seriously is to talk about it when you take yourself too seriously.

When you hear a laugh, move towards it. Often people are pleased to share something interesting. Because it allows them to laugh again and develop the humor, they find there. When you hear a laugh, give him a call and join in.

Spend time with people who are fun and playful. These are people who easily laugh at themselves and the absurdities of life and find humor in everyday events daily. Active perspectives and laughter are contagious.

Wrap yourself in a relaxing memory. Put the toy on yourdesk or in your car. Hang a fun poster in your office. Choose a computer screensaver that will make you laugh. A shot that shows you and your loved ones are having fun.

Take care of the children and imitate them. They are experts in gaming, making life more comfortable, and laughing.

Tip 7: Eat a Diet That Activates Your Brain

Just as the body demands fuel, so does the brain. As you already know, diets based on fruits, vegetables, whole grains, "healthy" fats (olive oil, nuts, fish, etc.), and lean proteins offer many health benefits. A good diet also improves memory. But for brain health, it's not only what you eat; it's also what you don't eat.

The following nutrition tips can help improve brain performance and reduce the risk of dementia.

- **Get Omega-3 Fatty Acids:** Studies show that omega-3 fatty acids are particularly beneficial for brain health. Fish is a particularly abundant source of omega-3 fatty acids, especially cold-water fatty fish, salmon, fish, halibut, trout, mackerel, sardines, and herring.

On the off chance that you aren't good with seafood, consider omega-3 fatty acids like seaweed, nuts, flaxseed oil, flaxseed oil, pumpkin, beans, beans, spinach, broccoli, pumpkin seeds, and soy.

- **Limit Calories and Saturated Fat:** Studies have shown that diets based on saturated fat (lean meat, whole milk, butter, cheese, cream, ice cream, etc.) increase the risk of dementia and impair concentration and memory.
- **Eat More Fruits and Vegetables:** This product is rich in antioxidants, protecting brain cells from damage. Ripe fruits and fresh vegetables are an excellent source of antioxidants, "super foods."
- **Drink Green Tea:** Green tea contains polyphenols, a powerful antioxidant that protects against free radicals that can damage brain cells. Among many other benefits, regular green tea intake

improves memory and mental alertness and slows down brain aging.

- **Drink moderate Wine (Or Grape Juice):** Alcohol kills brain cells, so it's essential to control alcohol consumption. Moderately (about 1 cup per day for women and 2 cups for men), alcohol can boost memory and cognition. The wine is materialized to be the best option because it is rich in resveratrol, a flavonoid that helps grow blood flow to the brain and reduce the risk of Alzheimer's disease. Other resveratrol-rich options include grape juice, cranberry juice, fresh grapes, berries, and peanuts.

Tip 8: Identify and Treat Health Problems

Does your memory seem like a mysterious depression? If so, there may be health and lifestyle issues. Dementia and Alzheimer's disease aren't the only causes of amnesia.

There are many diseases, mental disorders, and medications that can affect memory:

- **Heart condition and its risk factors:** Cardiovascular diseases such as hypercholesterolemia and hypertension and their risk factors are associated with tender cognitive impairment.

- **Diabetes:** Research shows that people with diabetes experience a much more significant cognitive decline than people without diabetes.
- **Hormonal imbalance:** Menopausal women often have memory problems when estrogen is low. In men, low testosterone levels can cause problems. Thyroid imbalances can also lead to forgetfulness, slowed thinking, or confusion.
- **Dosage:** Many recommendations and over-the-counter medications can interfere with memory and clear thinking. Common causes are colds, allergies, sleeping pills, and antidepressants. Inform your doctor or pharmacist about possible side effects.

Are you depressed?

Emotional problems can be just as stressful to the brain as physical problems. Mental dullness, low concentration, and forgetfulness are common symptoms of depression. Memory problems can be especially severe in older people with depression. Therefore, it can be mistaken for dementia. The good news is that treating depression should bring your memory back to normal.

Tip 9: Take Practical Steps to Help You Learn and Remember

Watch out. If you've never learned it, you don't remember anything. Also, without special attention, you can't know anything or code it in your brain. It takes about 8 seconds of concentration to process the information in your memory. If you get distracted easily, choose a quiet, undisturbed place.

Include as many sensations as possible. Try to associate information with color, texture, smell, and taste. By physically rewriting a story, you can shape it in your brain. Also, read aloud what you want to remember as you study visually. It would be even better if you could recite it rhythmically.

Connect the information to what you already learned. Link new data to information you already remember, whether it's new material based on previous knowledge or something simple as the address of someone living as you already know them.

For more complex materials, focus on understanding the basic idea rather than memorizing isolated details. Practice explaining your concepts to others in your own words.

Test the information you have already learned. Make sure you regularly knew on the same day that you learned. This "spaced trial" is more

effective than jamming, especially in retaining what you have learned.

Use a mnemonic device to facilitate memorization. A mnemonic (the first "m" is silent) is usually any clue that helps you remember something, helps you associate information you want to remember with a visual image, phrase, or word.

Six Types of Mnemonic Devices

1. **Visual Images**: Pair graphical photos with words and names to make them easier to remember.

   Positive, calming, vibrant, colorful, and stereoscopic images are easier to remember. Example: To remember Rosa Park's name and name recognition, imagine a woman sitting on a bench in a park surrounded by roses and waiting for the bus to stop.

1. **Acrostic (or Sentence):** Create a sentence in which each word's first letter is part of what you want to remember or represents its acronym. For example, the phrase "Every Nice Guy is okay" recalls the lines of the treble symbols that represent the notes E, G, B, D, and F.

2. **Acronyms** are words that consist of taking the first few letters of a keyword or idea that you need to remember and creating a new one. Example: Remember the names of the Great Lakes. The word "CASE": Huron, Ontario, Michigan, Erie, Superior.

3. **Alliteration and Alliteration:** Alliteration, alliteration (repeated sounds or syllables), and even jokes are memorable to remember more mundane facts and figures. Example: Remember the month of the year with only 30 days, with the rhyme "30th is September, April, June, November".

4. **Chunking:** Chunking breaks a long list of numbers and other types of information into smaller, more manageable chunks.

5. **Locating Method:** Imagine placing an object you want to remember along a familiar path or at a specific location in a

standard room or building. Example: For a shopping list, imagine a banana in the hallway, a puddle of milk in the center of the sofa, an egg climbing up the stairs, and bread on the bed.

PHOTOGRAPHIC MEMORY

The human brain can save and reproduce previously captured images, objects, phenomena, and circumstances in precise detail also called phenomenal memory. The word eidetic has Greek roots - "eidos." means image and appearance. Until now, eidetic in psychology is a genuinely inexplicable phenomenon of individuals, sometimes accompanied by excellent computing capabilities, superior to modern computers of the latest generation.

Is It Possible to Develop A Photographic Memory?

Photographic memory can be a congenital feature or an acquired method of systematic training. Psychologists explain that such memory allows the reproduction of past events in minute detail, where the base is the image. Still, other types of memory are connected - tactile, auditory, and even olfactory. The person reproduces the plot in his head as if the real situation were real.

Eidetic memory has the property of cutting past moments, replacing them with plots based on emotions experienced at that moment or experiences. Scientists say that photographic memory is inherent in everyone from early childhood, but it loses its properties over the years.

How to Quickly Develop a Photographic Memory?

To develop a Photographic memory at least to the famous

Sherlock Holmes level, we must make great efforts. Learn not to see only the image and shape to notice the smallest details. Thrall concentrated on the surrounding objects, taking into account the little things on a conscious level the first step towards super memory development. The formation and development of memory will first pass consciously; after a certain period, such study will go smoothly to an unconscious level.

Studying and reading the last day or movie seen in detail with the correct sequence should be done in mind every day - this will help develop this type of memory more quickly. A detailed analysis of the images by careful 30-second examination at the beginning of the training should be a systematic habit, a common occurrence. It is advisable to reduce the study interval after each successful period.

How to Develop Photographic Memory Exercises?

The formation of photographic memory is brain work; it should not remain inactive. An everyday activity for people who want to develop memory should be solving crosswords, puzzles, logic tasks, learning foreign languages - practicing neurotics. The brilliant Leonardo da Vinci developed his skills, studying the walls with a spray of paints, but modern technique suggests starting the exercises with elementary memorization tasks.

Select a paragraph from the book and try to study it, not read it cover to cover, and capture the entire text, like on a movie camera, to understand the meaning of the indicated information. It would be best if you started with small tasks. To check your skills on paper, a clear example will show the lost moments.

Similarly, training courses are carried out in numbers -

We have to ask someone to write a line or column with numbers, show it to us for a few seconds, note what was remembered on a piece of paper, and check with the original file.

It will help develop the ability to study formulas - mathematics, physics, or chemistry, regardless of the subject being studied.

View and check the information stored on a sheet of paper with an annotation.

Games for the Development of Photographic Memory

Games for the development of photographic memory contribute to the training of the brain's right hemisphere.

Tasks that develop photographic memory at any age:

- **Read back:** You should start with simple words, then form sentences and phrases.
- **Listen to someone else's conversation:** Being in a public place, you have to take an excerpt from someone else's conversation, and then reproduce all the words and intonation, you hear - to represent others' emotions.
- **They are making associations:** comparing objects and furniture with familiar objects.
- **The study of poetry helps develop memory:** When reading aloud with intonation and accent, the text should not seem monotonous; it should transmit thoughts and experiences.

Neurolinguistics Exercises for Memory

Do many people wonder what neurolinguistics is? You also ask yourself this same question, very well, you have to pay close attention to what I will tell you since you will learn what neurolinguistics is and some exercises that you can do for memory.

Neurolinguistics can be said that it is the tool that allows us to understand and analyze symbols, as well as words that could benefit us or in a certain way influence and alter our way of thinking and improve our behavior as well as it could influence our "memory system.". Negative feelings from memory can have lingering effects and cause unwanted stress on the body. Do many people wonder what neurolinguistics is? You also ask yourself the same question, very well; you have to pay close attention to what I will tell you since you will learn what neurolinguistics is and some exercises that you can do for memory.

How To Create

A Passive Income From Your Home

Become Your Own Boss,
Create Wealth And
Change Your Life

Kenneth C. Lorenz

Introduction

These days, anyone who has an internet connection and a computer or smartphone can begin making money fast. This is one of the wonderful things about this futuristic world we live in. With these tools, you can become your own boss and begin making an income from the comfort of your home. This book will teach you how to do this and set you up for success from the start!

This book will teach you everything you need to know and help you prevent making mistakes along the way. Take it from someone who has done it and who is somewhat of an expert in the field; making quick money is possible, and it's easier than you think!

What to Expect From This Book?

Throughout this book, I will teach you all the information and skills you need to begin making quick money! I will also teach you how to become a successful entrepreneur.

I will begin by teaching you about *passive income,* and you will learn about how this can be the key to financial freedom.

This book aims to help you create extra streams of income for yourself and turn them into consistent, growing income. The goal is to set you up so that you can eventually make enough money to make large, secure investments like purchasing a house or investing in stocks!

Throughout this book, you will find a plethora of examples of different methods for making quick money, as well as various business ideas that can provide you with passive income. This information will help you understand the difference between a part-time job and a side hustle and help you begin making passive income for yourself!

Continue reading if you want to find freedom from your day job and be your own boss! This book will help you develop a passive income source for yourself. It's never too late to begin saving for retirement or your next vacation! It's never too late to get out of debt once and for all!

Chapter 1: Things to Know Before You Begin

We will begin the book by defining several terms so that you can continue reading the following chapters with confidence! This chapter will teach you about passive income, online income, and the many benefits that come with them.

What is Passive Income?

Before we dive into the rest of this book, wherein we will discuss specific examples of ways to make quick money, I will begin by defining the term *passive income* for you.

Passive income is a type of income derived from a business or enterprise in which you are not actively involved.

On the other hand, *active income* is income paid to you in exchange for a series of services that you have performed. Examples of active income include; salaries, wages, commissions, tips, and business endeavors. Examples of this kind of income would be working as a teller at a bank. In this type of position, you would be paid in salary or hourly. You would be getting paid in exchange for the services you perform for that bank's daily operations. Another example would be a waiter working at a restaurant; their wages per hour are their active income, as are the tips they make. They actively perform services for one specific establishment and are an employee of the business.

As I mentioned, passive income is a type of income that comes from a business or enterprise where the person is not actively involved. Passive income may include income from a rental property, a company you have shares in, or renting out your car on share websites. Passive income is different from the types of jobs people usually spend their time on because passive income does not require nearly as many hours.

The Benefits of Making Extra Money Online

The best way to make extra money to supplement your salary is by getting yourself a *side hustle*. A side hustle is almost like a 'second-job' that provides you with another source of income. Rather than being employed by someone else or another company, a side hustle is a business that you opened yourself 'on the side' that is either your passion project or another method to help make you money.

With financial security becoming a considerable problem for nearly 50% of Americans, side hustles have become a popular option for people looking to get out of debt or are just interested in starting their own business.

The Difference Between a Traditional Job and an Online, Passive Income Source

You might be wondering why it matters which type of income you make when they both produce money for you in the end? Well, it matters because your ability to accomplish your financial goals depends on you understanding these two different terms.

In the simplest terms, active income (from a traditional job) means that you are physically doing something to obtain income. In contrast, passive income means you are 100% hands-off or close to it. Side hustles are not the same as a second job or a part-time job. Your employer will be managing your time and how much pay you receive for that time at a part-time job. On the other hand, side hustles give you the freedom to decide how much you want to earn and how many hours you want to work.

The Benefits of Passive Income

If you want to make enough money to help you save for your retirement or make investments, your day job salary may not be enough. The ideal situation is to provide yourself with a second income source that does not take up much of your time. This will speed up the process of achieving your life goals and will mean that you still have time to spend with your family or on the other areas of your life that require attention.

Challenges You May Face

While making extra income comes with many benefits, it will also come with some challenges. These challenges do not need to discourage you; instead, they can motivate you. It is important to understand the challenges you may face before they arise to be prepared to overcome them and bounce back.

It will require a lot of time and energy at the beginning.

You will build your side hustle during the hours outside of your day job as you get started. Due to this, your working hours for your side hustle will likely take place during weekends, evenings, or holidays.

The reason for this is because side hustles may not generate enough (or any) income until you get the proper traction and marketing to begin making money. Having a full-time job enables you to have the ability to pay your bills while also spending some of your free time building your side-hustle, so eventually, it does start creating a separate stream of income.

This will likely be an adjustment initially, but once you establish your side hustle of business, you will begin to see that you have more money and more time than ever before.

Employ the Right Mindset
Mindset is crucial when it comes to financial success and making quick money. The way you think and feel about money has everything to do with how you spend it and save it. People with negative mindsets towards money such as; "I never have enough of it anyway, might as well buy this new television now" or "If I don't spend it on something I like, the money will go elsewhere." Mindsets like this cause your finances to always get you stuck in a vicious cycle. Financially intelligent people typically have strong self-discipline. In many cases, self-discipline is the key to financial success.

Many researchers suggest that the most critical thing in a person's ability to become financially successful is their self-discipline level. Self-discipline is responsible for helping people stay focused on reaching their goals, giving them the grit that they need to stick with difficult tasks, and overcoming barriers and discomforts as they push themselves to achieve greater things. Let's refresh our memory on the definition of self-discipline. Self-discipline is the ability of a person to control their impulses, reactions, behaviors, and emotions. It allows them to let go of instant gratification in exchange for long-term gain and satisfaction. It's the act of saying no when you want to say yes. Self-discipline isn't about living a restrictive and boring life without any enjoyment. It's almost impossible to be 100% self-disciplined in every single area of your life. Rather than trying to be disciplined at everything you do, you can use it to focus on the most important things.

As you begin your journey to creating your side hustle, it is important to recognize that you will likely face some obstacles. By accepting this fact before they arise, you will not be surprised, but rather you will feel prepared.

Before you begin, take some time to write in your journal about what some possible obstacles may be. Once you have done this, take some time to plan and decide how you will deal with them when they arise so that they do not disrupt your progress or cause you to resort to old ways that are unhealthy.

By setting yourself up for success in this way, you will be able to tackle any challenge without having your new lifestyle jeopardized.

Chapter 2: Dropshipping and E-Commerce

Our first discussion of lucrative and quick income sources is something called *Dropshipping* and *E-Commerce*. Let's dive into the different ways that you can begin to make money using online stores.

What is Dropshipping?

Dropshipping is a relatively new business model that people can use to run lucrative online stores. Dropshipping is simple; essentially, you have your online store with items of your choice to sell. You also have a relationship with a wholesaler that can sell your products at wholesale prices.

You could sell items including watches, mugs, clothing, electronics, and anything else you can dream of. Once a customer purchases an item from your store, you will then purchase your item from the wholesaler and have the wholesaler mail that item to your customer directly. You don't have to hold any inventory in your home with Dropshipping, and you don't have to make many items from scratch.

You also benefit from not having to pre-buy inventory, so you minimize the risk of producing a loss. What I mean by this is the traditional way to run an online store is to have an inventory for things, right?

For instance, let's say you wanted to run an online watch business, and you bought ten watches for this season at the cost of $15 each. However, by the end of the season, you only sold five watches at $40 each. Selling your items in this way means that you spent $150 on your inventory and only made $200; that's $50 profit, and you are left with five watches that are now out of season.

Dropshipping allows you to minimize your risk of having leftover, unsellable product by purchasing items and selling them as the orders come in, therefore, maximizing your profit and minimizing risk. In the same example of watches, if you only had five orders for that season and bought five watches as those orders came in, you have made a $125 profit compared to the measly $50 profit.

Numerous online platforms allow you to utilize the Dropshipping method. Some examples include;

Shopify
Shopify is a very popular Dropshipping platform that is increasing in popularity each year. Shopify helps users by connecting them with suppliers who will ship the products to their customers directly.

Shopify has two options for sellers:

1. Shopify will connect you with North American or Asian suppliers who can fulfill your orders as they come in.
2. Shopify can help you by connecting you to online suppliers like AliExpress or Amazon, who can fulfill your orders for you.

With the first option, you will likely be connected with a supplier specializing in the products you are looking to sell. With the second option, you will be connected with a marketplace that carries and sells every product under the sun.

The potential is limitless when it comes to these kinds of online stores, and the best part is that you do not need to hold onto any stock to run your store!

Alibaba.com

Alibaba.com is another method for Dropshipping. Alibaba is similar to Amazon in that it sells virtually anything you can imagine for affordable prices. With Alibaba, you can sell any products that they carry to customers, and you remain virtually hands-off throughout the entire process. Alibaba will ship the order to your customer, and you collect the money while paying a cut to Alibaba.

Other Examples of E-Commerce Income Sources

We will now learn a little about online stores, how they can be great side gigs and some of their benefits.

Online stores are similar to popular e-platforms like Amazon and eBay. However, the ones that can be utilized as side-gigs are typically on a smaller scale where sellers can post items they've made or second-hand items up for sale. There are numerous amounts of online store platforms that are extremely user-friendly and can help you make money by selling your old items or hand-made items.

Print On Demand

Print On Demand (POD) E-Commerce is similar to Dropshipping, but it requires your artistic and design abilities. What POD entails is selling prints that you have designed. The products could range from your paintings, drawings, graphic design, etc. You are then selling your designs printed on items of the customers' choice like posters, phone cases, t-shirts, tapestries, and many other options. You can choose only to sell one form of a product like specifically phone cases, or you can sell your designs on any imaginable printable surface. POD is ideal for someone who has a strong artistic ability to create designs. Depending on the popularity of your art, this can be a business with extremely high earning potential.

The costs simply consist of the items you want to print on (e.g., t-shirts, phone cases) and a company to do the actual printing itself. For instance, if a printing company agrees to print your design for $10 on a t-shirt and the t-shirt costs $5, the total cost for your t-shirt + design is $15. If you are selling those shirts for $40, you are bringing in $25 of profit. Again, the great part about this is similar to drop shipping; you only have to pay for the cost of the orders WHEN you get the orders. Paying upon order prevents you from holding a stock of different sized t-shirts with different prints, which will cost you a fortune if the business is slow. You only need to pay for costs when you get an actual order, which will guarantee your profit. Platforms that support this type of online store include Printful.com, Printify.com, and Teespring.com.

As a creative person, this side gig is highly beneficial for creating and selling tees or merchandise you create. This option is especially beneficial for those who may already pursue creative endeavors, such as if you are a musician, for example. That way, you can sell merchandise for your band.

If you already have an online platform that markets your work, it is good to add an online store to do POD business. You can sell your band logo and album covers in the form of t-shirts and other merchandise! Having multiple stores can increase your streams of passive income. That way, you still have plenty of time to pursue other side gigs to make you money.

Etsy
If you have artistic talent and have hobbies making art, running your own Etsy online store is an amazing option for you. For instance, if you have a hobby in making pottery and have gotten a lot of praise for your work, you can start your own Etsy store by selling pottery items that you have made in the past and open yourself up to commission pieces as well. Etsy is a fantastic way to make money if you are already doing your hobby regardless if it makes you money or not. You can have fun and improve your artistic ability while making some cash.

The earning potential for this is difficult to calculate as it highly depends on how successful your sales are and how you are pricing your items. For example, let's say you like to make mugs when you are doing pottery, and you make around five mugs per week. If you sold them on Etsy for $25 each and managed to sell 4 per week, you are making around $100/week and $400/month. Again, it's not a huge amount of income if your Etsy store isn't making huge sales. Still, it's good money considering that this is your hobby, and you were going to make these items anyway.

How to Use These Methods to Make Quick Money

The first benefit that comes with using online stores as your side gig is time. You don't have to invest a lot of time into it; all you need to do to get started on most of these platforms are the following:

1. Simply make an account.
2. Begin with a few items that you'd like to sell
3. Make a post
4. Reply to the interested people.

Yes, it's that simple. However, you have to keep in mind that some items receive more attention from customers than others. For instance, Apple products or any type of decently new electronics tend to get a lot of online attention. These products do well on second-hand online platforms like Letgo, Craigslist, and eBay. If you are artistically skilled and can make homemade crafts like jewelry, pottery (mugs, vases, bowls), knits, etc., you can utilize more specialized websites like Etsy.

What Costs Are Associated?

Like any other platform that we discussed in this book, you will need to pay a cut of your profits to the businesses that help you complete your orders. For example, if you have a Shopify site that hosts your store, you will need to pay them a cut of your revenue. If you use Alibaba.com to complete your orders, you will need to pay them a cut.

For example, Shopify charges sellers 2.9% plus an additional 30 cents for each transaction that your site gets. Additionally, there is a $29 monthly fee for Shopify Basic, a $79 fee for The Shopify Plan, and a $299 fee for Advanced Shopify. Each plan comes with its own set of benefits, so you will likely choose a plan according to how well your site is doing.

How Much Money Can You Expect to Make?

Dropshipping can provide you with very quick, very easy income if you know how to gain traction on your site. Imagine that you have a Shopify store where you sell watches to customers for $40. Your wholesaler sells you watches for $15. Because of this difference in cost and sale price, you make $25 of profit for every watch. The profit that you make will depend on what you are selling and what the demand is like.

When running a business, your profit is the result of your revenue, minus your costs. So, your net profit margin, otherwise known as the "bottom line," is the revenue (in dollars) remaining once every expense and type of income is calculated. This amount will include the operational expenses, the cost of the goods you are selling, and any other expenses such as taxes, debts, and other payments. This number reflects a business's ability to generate profit from its income. This number will become important to you as you begin your business, as it will help you keep track of how well your business is doing. This number will also help you to determine when you can transition from your day job to a full-time business owner.

Before we begin the next chapter, I kindly ask that if you like this book and think that others would also enjoy the information contained within these pages, please leave us a positive review on Amazon! Your kind words will go a long way in helping us get this carefully researched information across to as many people as possible!

Chapter 3: Content Writing and Self-Publishing

Content writing and self-publishing are great ways to make money on the side, in addition to your regular day job. Let's take a look at some of these methods and how you can utilize them to make quick money. In terms of flexibility, freelance writing work is extremely flexible since you can do it anywhere and anytime. Let's begin.

What is Content Writing?

Overall, there are numerous ways that you can make money in the realm of content creation. Content creation can include anything from creating unique videos, audio, or articles to writing business pieces for companies.

The Content Writing Industry includes many different types of writing jobs, including business writing, educational article writing, and copywriting. More specifically, the content you could write includes company blogs, LinkedIn articles, product review articles, and specific niche blogs. The side jobs within this category are specialized within the business writing industry. This includes any types of company blogs, LinkedIn articles, and e-books.

How to Make Quick Money Online Through Content Writing

When it comes to side gigs in content creation, content writing is a great choice. There are a few platforms that help connect content writers to businesses and people that require this talent.

One way to generate income from writing is to start your own independent writing side gig. This method is more elaborate than utilizing platforms to connect you to clients as it requires you to find your clients and pitch your skills based on your needs. You can do this by developing a strong sales pitch that consists of your experience, writing skills, and an explanation of why you are a good candidate for the job. Businesses tend to look for people who can write articles, books, and white papers.

There is a TON of undiscovered business in this area, and all it takes to tap into a steady and high source of side gig income is finding the right client who trusts in your skills. One method to approach finding clients is looking for Content Managers or businesses on LinkedIn and reaching out to them. Try to choose businesses that you know require writers.

To generate business, it is a numbers game. The more people you reach out to with your services, the more likely you will get a hit. Do this at least 100 times a day with different businesses and positions of people; you will likely get some hits back to learn more about what you can offer. The best part about this method is that it has high earning potential if you can find yourself a handful of steady clients. However, if luck isn't on your side, this is not a steady income source as you have to spend hours reaching out to people and pitching your services, and you could end up not having much return on it. This method's flexibility is very high; as I said, you can write anywhere and anytime. The hardest part about making this side gig method work is getting the clients, to begin with.

What is Self-Publishing?

Self-publishing is a quickly emerging industry that gives people the potential to make large sums of money very quickly. Self-publishing is done when a person publishes their works by themselves without using a publishing company. In this way, publishing allows the person to maintain ownership of all profits and royalties made by their work. If your book or piece of work makes large sums of money, you do not have to pay part of your profits to the publishing company that helped you, which is why this is such an attractive income source.

With the emergence of the internet, this has become a much more accessible way to make money than it used to be since you can self-publish in an e-book or online format instead of publishing in paper format. Below, we will look at the most popular form of self-publishing material, the e-book.

E-Book Self-Publishing
There are a few different ways to make money through self-publishing, both active and passive. We will look at these methods below.

1. One great way to benefit from content writing in a passive form is by writing books or writing pieces and uploading them to various locations, which will earn you money when people pay to read them. For example, if you write an e-book, you can sell it on amazon or other e-book hosting locations. This way, your book will make money each time someone buys it, and this provides you with passive income.

2. Another way is to write e-books for an online company. That way, you get paid to write the books, but you do not have to concern yourself with the business's advertising or customer side.

3. The third way to earn extra money from E-Books is by getting other people to write your books for you and then giving them a cut of the profit when people purchase the book.

Each of these three methods has its own benefits and drawbacks, but they are all good options for making money through content writing. We will look at some of the best platforms for self-publishing in the following section.

Amazon Kindle Direct Publishing (KDP)

KDP or Kindle Direct Publishing is a section of Amazon where you can self-publish e-books. You can use this part of Amazon to either publish books that you have written or to publish books that someone has written for you, depending on which type of e-book creation source you choose to go with.

Kindle Direct Publishing is a hub where people can download e-books straight to their smartphone or Kindle e-reader. Kindle represents the future of reading books, and it has created quite a name for itself over the past ten years. KDP allows you to self-publish by getting your book out there for people across the world to see, something that would have been very difficult in the past. These days, anyone could stumble across your book, and before you know it, you could be a household name.

Amazon allows you to create an author page that contains links to your books, reviews, and a little bit of information about you. This way, if you have multiple books, people can find them all in one place. Additionally, not only can you sell e-books, but you can also sell print books from this page if your readers prefer to have a book in-hand.

Like we discussed in our Dropshipping chapter, Amazon KDP boasts a print-on-demand service, where the book will be printed when a person places the order. This presents new opportunities for income if you are a writer since you do not need to pay to have your books printed upfront, which means there are much fewer overhead costs.

How Much Money Can You Expect to Make?

Content writing side gigs require some time to ramp up as they are highly dependent on how well your content does in the marketplace. However, the profit generated from this type of work can be extremely high (we're talking over thousands per month), and therefore, people who have talent and skill in this area may be interested in this type of work.

You can always work in content writing as one of your income sources and have steadier sources that generate your income while ramping up your content. This way, you are not going without making any money, but you are still allowing yourself to generate income through creating content. Then, when your content writing picks up traction in the online marketplace, you can increase the amount of time you spend on it. The earning potential is high once you gain recognition and a name for yourself in the industry.

If you self-publish with Amazon KDP, you will keep around 70% of the profits of each book you sell. This is great when compared to authors who publish with a traditional publishing company and is one of the great benefits of self-publishing. One drawback is that if your book costs any amount over ten dollars, you will only make 35% of the profit, so keep this in mind when writing and pricing your books.

Chapter 4: Online Advertising Income

In this chapter, we will look at ways to create a side gig for yourself online by taking advantage of the world of advertising dollars! There are many ways to do this, and in this chapter, I will outline the options available to you.

Online advertising money is given to people who create content that people enjoy. This content can include videos, pictures, or anything that you can post on the internet that will get large numbers of people's attention. There is a great market for content creation advertising today since the internet and social media have such a massive presence in our society.

If you can take advantage of this, you can provide yourself with an income source by merely posting content on the internet. Once you develop a following for yourself, you can begin to make money by giving this following with pictures and videos of yourself. You will get paid through advertising and views, which is an excellent way to make passive income.

We will begin by looking at the different options you have to put your content up for everyone to see.

Social Media Income for Your Business

Social media is a relatively new way to make money since it used to be used solely to connect with friends. Still, now every business has multiple social media accounts- one on every platform. Businesses and brands use these social media accounts to reach consumers and advertise their products. These days, there are advertisements on social media news feeds so that people see them as they are scrolling through their timeline, looking at the people they follow, and product placement in the posts of people with many followers like celebrities or models.

This type of income is not just for celebrities, though; you can use this method if you are starting or running a business. You can make income by attracting new customers through social media, or you can make money with product placement deals on your business social media accounts.

There are several social media platforms, including Instagram, Facebook, Twitter, Twitch, Tumblr, and so on. All of these platforms have the potential to make you money if you have a large following, which results in lots of "likes" on your content or millions of views on your videos. The best way to maximize your following is to cross over your social media accounts, advertising one platform on the other, so that your followers can follow you on every platform possible.

With social media, the earning potential is pretty much unlimited, though you have to reach the social media celebrity level to begin earning a lot of money. If you have around 10 thousand followers, you can begin to get partnerships with brands that will give you free merchandise or up to $150. The money begins to flow when your social media following reaches one million followers. Then, you can begin to make 15 thousand US dollars for a single post! Any number of followers in between will give you some money between $150 and $15 000. A big range, I know. But it depends on the number of partnerships you have and the brands which are paying you to advertise their product for them.

In addition to having a lot of likes and views, there are some other ways that you can make money using social media. Some of these ways are outlined below.

Social Media Management

The first way we will look at is Social Media Management. Social media management is when you manage all of your social media accounts and organize what you will post to maximize your potential reach and visibility.

Hootsuite

Hootsuite is a social media management tool that you can use to manage all of your social media accounts on a single screen. You can include your Facebook, LinkedIn, Twitter, Instagram, and YouTube accounts and keep up with them from one place. In addition to monitoring your likes and views, Hootsuite allows you to schedule your posts so that you can keep your accounts active throughout the day while you are busy or while you are on vacation away from your computer. Hootsuite also allows you to keep track of your reach and the attention your posts get and graph them so that you can compare your results over time.

There is a single place where you can view your comments, your mentions, and where you were tagged and reply straight from the Hootsuite interface. You will also receive notifications from all connected social media accounts so you can keep on top of what is going on in each of them without becoming overwhelmed by having to flip back and forth between apps on your phone.

Hootsuite works on a membership basis, so you must pay a monthly fee if you wish to use their services. This fee and more can be returned to you, however, with the money you have made on your social media platforms as they grow in popularity.

SproutSocial

Another social media management tool is SproutSocial. This social media management platform is similar to Hootsuite. It allows you to have all of your social media accounts in one place. SproutSocial has different tabs within its home page for different aspects of your social media management. It contains a tab for Publishing, where you can control your posts and schedule them, a tab for Analytics where you can track your activity, and a tab for Engagement to monitor your comments and respond to them straight from the SproutSocial page. With SproutSocial, you can link your Facebook, Twitter, LinkedIn, Instagram, TripAdvisor, and Pinterest too.

Crowdfunding Income

Utilizing a fan base that you already have is a great way to develop a side hustle while still working on your other projects! This side gig is ideal for business owners, musicians, or artists, as you don't have to step away from your day job to make quick, extra money. This section will provide you with some examples of platforms designed to help you turn your fan base into dollars.

Patreon

The first platform we will look at is called Patreon. This platform is a way for your fans to stay connected with you and access content that they otherwise wouldn't be able to see. They can use this platform to keep up to date on your behind the scenes, your exclusive content, or your yet-to-be-released products that they want to be the first ones to access.

This platform runs on a membership basis, which means your fans will pay a monthly fee to stay connected with you. There are different membership tiers, which all include different benefits. Your fans can choose which membership tier they want to subscribe to, which informs their monthly fee.

For example, your first tier of membership can include access to a community group chat as well as a free mp3 download. Your second tier can include these things as well as access to a monthly live video chat. Deciding on your tiers and what each of them includes is up to you!

Because this platform works on a monthly membership basis, your monthly revenue will be more predictable than it would with some other types of side gigs. Fans can add specific things to their monthly fees, such as merchandise or products that you sell.

On this platform, you also have the option to include ads on your page or any other sponsorship content that you may choose, which means that you can incorporate other streams of income on your page.

Wondering how much you can earn using Patreon? Imagine your business has a social media following of 30 thousand subscribers. Out of these 30 thousand people, you could say that about 15% of those are hardcore fans or followers. The membership rates often range from $5 to $25, and the highest ones are somewhere around $100. As a result, if somewhere between 45 and 230 people are subscribers of your page on Patreon, you can hope to make between $300 and $1600 monthly, depending on the number of fans that you have engaged in your monthly plans. Patreon takes about 2.5% of the membership sales to keep its platform running.

This platform allows you to connect with your fans in a closer way, as it does not use algorithms in the same way that social media platforms do. Often, on places like Instagram, your fans may miss content from you simply because of things like what they viewed last for what they view most. With Patreon, they will never miss content from you as there is no tricky algorithm that you have to workaround.

The above methods are great ways to keep doing what you love and creating your music without sacrificing it to pay your bills. These methods are great options for people who just aren't comfortable spending more time on their side gig than their creative endeavors, as this type of side gig combines both!

Chapter 5: Trading, Investing, and Cryptocurrency

In this chapter, we will discuss the numerous ways that you can grow the money you have saved up so that it builds your wealth without much effort from you. This chapter contains a lot of valuable information, so be sure to bookmark it so that you can return to it over and over again.

The Benefits

I will begin this chapter by informing you about some of the benefits of investing and trading. Investing in a general sense is beneficial for a variety of reasons. Firstly, it allows you to grow the money you have earned much quicker than you can make it.

Imagine it would take you ten years to make $20000 in savings by putting some money from every paycheck into a savings account. Instead of making 20 thousand dollars in this way, you could invest five thousand dollars today and see it grow to 20 thousand dollars in much less time than ten years. Also, by the time you have saved $20000, the impact of inflation would mean that your 20 thousand dollars would not be able to buy you nearly as much as it would today.

This sum of money could come from your savings account, or it could be a sum of money that you make working on your side job. One great option is to take the money you make from your secondary income source and use it to invest. That way, you are still living on your day job salary and are potentially growing a large sum of money on the side.

In addition to the benefits above, investment funds can provide you with numerous other benefits, including the following:

- You can maintain control over your shares in the company or asset that you have invested in.
- The fees related to investing will be much lower when investing in investment funds than if you were to invest your money on your own.
- Your funds are managed by professionals, taking some of the work out of it for you, allowing you to rest easier than investing yourself.
- Gives you more opportunities for investing because the investment funds are shared amongst many people, allowing for more selection.

Trading vs. Investing

Trading and investing. You have likely heard of these two terms before, but do you understand the differences between them? Before we look at specific examples of investments that you can pursue, we will first learn about the differences between trading and investing.

Trading is what people do with stocks. You have likely heard of Day Traders- people who spend their days buying and trading stocks. These people aim to buy stocks at a low price and sell them at a high price, leading to profit. This can be an extremely lucrative form of income, but it comes with high risk and a requirement to understand the stock market inside and out.

On the other hand, investing involves putting money into capital and leaving that money in place for an extended period. For example, purchasing a property and holding onto it while the market value increases. This is different from trading because it does not involve the same quick buying and selling. We will look at examples of each below so that you can better understand the differences. For now, though, you must understand that neither is better than the other, only that they are two options available to you.

The Basics of Trading and Investing

To understand trading and investing, we must first understand a few technical terms. Before defining what *investment funds* are, I must define the term *capital* for you.

Capital is a term used to describe assets. In this case, these assets are of the financial type. Financial assets can include the following:

- Cash
- Funds from financing
- Funds in deposit accounts
- Securities
- Cash equivalents

Now that you understand what capital is, I will define investment funds for you. Investment funds are a type of capital that is held by many investors at the same time. These investors all maintain ownership of their shares of the capital.

Types of Trading That you Can Pursue

Now that you understand trading and investing, we will look at examples of each to give you a better idea of your options.

Stocks

Stocks are one of the most basic investment forms and likely the most common one you hear about. In the most basic explanation, stocks are securities that represent an ownership share in a company. Companies will issue stocks to raise money from the general public to grow and invest in their own business. Stocks are then exchanged in the stock market. The stock market, such as the New York Stock Exchange, is made up of exchanges. Stocks are listed on a specific exchange and allow sellers and buyers to come together to sell/buy shares of certain stocks. The exchange tracks the supply and demand, which usually directly relates to the price or each stock.

Stock prices fluctuate daily, and people who own stocks hope that stocks that they own will increase in value with time. For instance, if you bought a stock for company A for $20 apiece, and that stock grows to be worth $50 apiece in three years, you have made $30 over three years ($10 per year). However, stocks carry some of the highest risks than other investments, but they can also reap higher rewards. Some people look at stocks as a type of 'gambling' as it is difficult to predict the increase/decrease of stocks. Take a look at bitcoin; for example, what used to be a $7 stock grew to be worth $7000 per stock in the past few years. Although this may sound promising, it can happen the other way around too. You can buy a bitcoin stock for $7000 now and hope that it will grow to $14,000 or more. However, it could drop down back to $7, causing you to lose significant amounts of money.

Exchange-Traded Fund (ETF)

An ETF (exchange-traded fund) is a type of investment fund that involves several securities like stocks. This group of securities follows a common theme.

Investment Options

We will now learn about several investment options available to you today.

Bonds

Unlike a stock, a bond is a kind of loan that a company takes out, but instead of asking the bank for this money, they ask investors for money by asking them to purchase bonds. As an exchange for the capital, the company will pay an annual interest rate on the bond, annually or semiannual, and then return the principal loan when it reaches maturity.

There are six features that you should look out for before purchasing a bond:

- **Maturity:** Maturity refers to the date when the bond is paid, and when the initial chunk of money is returned to you. Maturity is often divided up into; short-term (1 – 3 years), medium-term (10+ years), and long-term (20+ years)

- **Secured/unsecured:** This term describes the fact that a bond can either be secured or unsecured.

A secured bond promises the bondholders certain assets in the event that the company is unable to repay the money. The term can also be described as "collateral." If the firm cannot pay back its money, then the agreed-upon asset will go to the lender.

Unsecured bonds are the opposite. Any collateral does not back them up. These bonds will return only a small portion of the initial investment that you made if the company cannot pay back the money.

- **Liquidation Preference:** When a company declares bankruptcy, it will repay its investors following a specific order as they liquidate their assets. Senior debt is what the company will repay first, and junior debt will be paid last. Stockholders will then get the remaining money if there is any.

- **Coupon:** This term is used to describe the amount of interest that the company pays to bondholders on either an annual or semiannual basis. The Coupon can be referred to as the nominal yield or the 'coupon rate.' To calculate this, divide your annual payments by the face value of your bond.

- **Tax Status:** Most corporate bonds are included in taxable investments, but if the bonds are municipal or government bonds, they will be tax-exempt. Any income or gains will be taxed. However, tax-exempt bonds will have a lower interest rate than taxable bonds.

- **Callability:** The company can pay off some bonds before its maturity. A company sometimes wishes to "call" the bonds if the interest rate allows for better borrowing rates.

Real Estate Investment Trust (REIT)
REIT stands for Real Estate Investment Trust. A REIT is a type of business that operates, finances or owns real estate that generates income for them. REITs are modeled similarly to the way that mutual funds operate, in that they pool capital from several different investors. This type gives investors dividends because the company can buy various real estate investments. The investor themselves does not need to buy, finance, or manage any of these properties on their own.

Typical properties in a REIT portfolio include hotels, apartment complexes, healthcare facilities, data centers, or can include telecommunications such as; fiber cables and cellphone towers. REITs also require a bit more knowledge in real-estate real estate as some REIT portfolios are a mixed bag of different properties. I don't recommend REITs for beginner investors as there are many risk factors and areas where you must learn about. However, many professional investors and traders swear by REITs, so if this is something you'd like to do, please do some heavy research and learn about the REITs in your market before investing any money.

Target-Risk Fund (TRF)

This kind of investment is a type of investment that involves a portfolio of a mix of stocks, bonds, and other types of investments. This type provides the investor with a varied mix of investments in one package.

Low-Cost Funds

Lost cost funds are an investment option for those who do not want to part with large amounts of money upfront. This kind of investment is a great option for risk-averse individuals, as these funds do not involve a person managing them, resulting in lower fees for investors.

Hedge Fund

A hedge fund is an investment company that people provide their money with to invest in. These hedge funds use the investors' money to purchase stocks or bonds while trying to beat the market or make experimental investments.

Commodities

Commodities are part of an average American's life each day. In its simplest form, a commodity includes a good that can be used in commerce to interchange with other goods in the same category. For example, grains, beef, gold, natural gas, and oil are traditional commodities.

Commodities are an important way for investors to add variety into their portfolios past the included traditional securities. Since commodity prices usually shift opposite the stocks, investors most often rely on commodities during market volatility periods. Professional traders usually do commodity trading as it is more complicated and does require quite a bit of knowledge and education to pull off effectively. For that reason, I won't go into detail about how commodities are traded and the functions.

Income Potential

With investing and trading, it is difficult to come up with a range of income potential. This is because the amount you can make depends on the amount that you invest or trade. For example, the more money you have, the more stock shares you can purchase. The more stock shares you purchase, the more money you have the potential to make if the value of those shares increases. For this reason, it is highly dependent on several factors. To get a better idea of this, I recommend speaking to a broker who can help you decide how to invest your money.

Risk

In the world of investing, things are changing by the second. There will always be a risk component involved in investing and trying to grow your wealth. There is no guarantee that you will succeed, but many people decide that the potential gain is worth the risk.

Every person who invests their money could see vastly different results from each other, depending on so many factors. You must remember that there is no "one size fits all" approach to investing. As long as you prepare yourself by learning the required information to prepare yourself, there is not much more that you can do. In the world of investing, there are no mathematical certainties, only risk, and reward.

With that being said, it is up to you to decide which risks you are willing to take and which you are not. Nobody else can decide for you, and nobody can predict the outcome. Keep this in mind as you begin investing your money. I wish you luck!

What is Cryptocurrency?

Another great way to make quick money online and one that fits into the umbrella of trading and investing is something called Cryptocurrency. You have likely heard of Bitcoin before, but do you know what it is? In this section, I will explain Cryptocurrency and how to use it to make money.

At its most basic level, Cryptocurrency is a digital form of currency. You can use this digital currency to buy things, like services or goods, and then sell them for a profit. One great way to understand Cryptocurrency is by thinking about it, like the tokens or tickets that you buy when you go to the fair or the casino. You need to pay money to buy this form of currency, which you then exchange for gameplay or a ride.

There are many different types of Cryptocurrency, Bitcoin being only one example. Other examples include *Chainlink, Ethereum,* and *Tether.*

There are also many benefits to using Cryptocurrency, namely the absence of banks controlling the money, which means that instead of decreasing in value over time (like when you keep money in a savings account), this currency can increase in value over time. Additionally, people are turning to Cryptocurrency for its digital security.

How to Make Money Using Cryptocurrency

One way to make money by using Cryptocurrency is to buy it and resell it at a higher value. This is similar to investing in a property and waiting for its value to increase before selling.

To do this, you will need to have a lump sum of money to purchase the Cryptocurrency, but once you do, you are likely to make money in the future as each currency unit's value increases.

Some people consider this to be a risky investment, so do some research and choose before you invest.

Chapter 6: Income Using Amazon

In this chapter, we will discuss how you can use Amazon to make an income. We have touched on this throughout the book so far, but we will discuss it in more detail.

Similar to Shopify, as we discussed in our Dropshipping chapter, Amazon can also provide you with a simple and easy way to sell products to customers all over the world. In addition to their Dropshipping services, Amazon also offers Amazon FBA, which we will look at below.

What is Amazon FBA?

Amazon FBA stands for "Fulfillment by Amazon." This is a service that Amazon provides to businesses who want to use their warehouses, packaging, and delivery services. For example, imagine that you are a business that sells computer parts. If you were to conduct business on your own without the help of Amazon, you would need to pay the following:

- to rent a warehouse to store your products
- purchase packing materials
- pay people to package your products when you get orders

- pay services to deliver your products to your customers.

Instead of doing this, you can use Amazon FBA, and all you need to do is send them your products to keep a stock on-hand for you. This way, your customers can put their orders in through the Amazon website, and they will receive their product the next day (if they subscribe to Amazon Prime) packaged neatly in an Amazon box.

How to Use It to Make Income

This method makes your income by eliminating the costs of storing and shipping for you. Depending on your products' size, you may require a lot of space and many shipping materials to get your products to your customers. Since Amazon is a force in terms of their packing and shipping quality and speed, allowing them to take care of it for you could save you money, thus increasing your profits.

Additionally, Amazon will take care of the customer service side of things, so you can spend your time and money focusing on other things. This way, you do not need to hire customer service representatives or spend time taking care of this yourself.

Resources You Need to Begin

To get started with Amazon FBA, you need the following resources:

- Product in-hand, ready to ship to Amazon Warehouses
- A business name and contact information
- Enough money to create more product if needed and to pay the Amazon monthly fee (if that is the plan you choose)

To get started with Amazon FBA, you don't need too much, especially since they can take their charges from your first order. This is a great option if you have a product ready to go and you have a little bit of money to start you off.

Costs Associated

There are some costs associated with using Amazon FBA, such as warehouse storage space usage and the fees that Amazon takes from each order for using their services. These fees range depending on the package that you choose.

For example, their cheapest plan will cost you 0.99 cents USD per unit of product that you sell. If you sell many units, you may instead opt for the Professional Plan, which costs $39.99 USD per month, for unlimited unit sales. Additionally, Amazon charges between 8 and 15% per item you sell as a fee for their website and advertising services (called a referral fee).

Profit Potential

Using Amazon FBA can provide you with some high income, depending on how many units you sell. For example, imagine that you sell 100 units of your product in one month. Imagine that you make $10 on each unit of your product sold. If you choose the Professional Plan, it will cost you $39.99 for the month to ship unlimited orders to your customers. If Amazon takes around 8% of your profits, this will leave you with about $885 in profit that month.

This is a rough estimate, but if you are running this business on the side, considering that it does not require much effort on your part, $885 USD of additional income is a great bonus to your day job salary.

Chapter 7: Online Freelance Jobs

This chapter will focus on secondary income sources that will allow you to use skills you may already have. Depending on which skills you have, they can prove extremely beneficial for freelance work. We will begin with consulting before moving onto freelance work.

Online Consulting Platforms

Consulting is an excellent option for people who have educated, excellent and sound advice to give others in specific areas, depending on your expertise.

Consulting can be a great side gig for those looking to have flexible hours and earn good money while still having time to do the other things they need to do in life. Depending on your background, there are different forms of consulting that you may be able to pursue. We will look at some of these below. We will also discuss specific platforms that you can use to get started if you wish to begin consulting on the side.

Clarity. FM

Clarity is an online consulting platform that connects experts with people looking to get advice on business-related topics such as Marketing, Social Media, and

243

Entrepreneurship, among others. If you have knowledge and experience relating to these areas, you may begin making money by sharing this advice with other people! If you are naturally somewhat of an entrepreneur, you may have the skills to become an expert with clarity. The great thing about clarity is that it has the flexibility to allow you to be an expert in a wide variety of topics within the larger umbrellas of Sales & Marketing, Technology, Skills & Management, and Product & Design. Within these umbrellas are a wide range of topics, and many people can find topics within these that they are knowledgeable in and confident giving advice in.

To begin earning money, you sign up as An Expert, and once you go through the onboarding process, you can begin having calls with people seeking your advice. You will get paid by the minute, so you are cashing in for each minute you spend on a call with a person seeking your advice. Most people charge between $2 and $7 per minute, depending on their experience, while the occasional expert will charge $50 to $80 per minute. This all depends on what type of experience and education you bring to the table. Experts set their rates, and choosing what rate to set will depend on your ability to show value. By starting somewhere around $1.60 per minute, your 30-minute call will get you $50. Based on this, you can decide what to charge. Clarity pays their experts every 15 days through

PayPal, and 15% of your pay is given to the company.

The majority of people who use clarity for advice purposes are new entrepreneurs or business owners looking to filter out all of the free advice they can find online and get real expert advice fast. By doing a quick search on the platform, you can find experts ready to advise on a vast range of topics, including the music industry.

Inzite.com

Inzite.com is another consulting platform that provides its users with advice on various topics through the use of consultants who are experts in their field. On Inzite, the consultants are called Advisors, and the advice-seekers are called Users. Inzite includes a wide variety of experts, including coaches, mentors, and consultants, who can offer support in any area of expertise when combined. Like Clarity, Inzite offers advice on a wide range of topics, music being one of them as there is an entire section of their Discover page titled "Arts, Music & Culture." If you are experienced in any specific area with advice to give, this could be a great solution for your side gig.

As an Advisor on Inzite, you can set your availability to let people know when you are available for meetings. The meetings come in the form of phone calls, instant messaging, and video chats. You have the option to offer free initial information sessions or to begin with paid sessions. To become an Advisor, you simply complete an online application form through their website. You hear back once the application has been processed.

Most calls work on a fixed-price basis, as the duration of the call will be pre-determined. You can decide on your fixed prices for pre-determined call lengths (30min, 45 min, etc.), or you can set an hourly rate that the user would pay by the minute. If the call goes overtime, the user is charged your per-minute rate. Inzite does not have subscription fees for its Advisors' users, but it takes 15% of your earnings. The calls are free of charge as they happen on a conference line set up by the platform. Your funds are deposited into your account on the platform, after which you can withdraw them into your bank account free of charge.

COMATCH.com
COMATCH is a consulting platform that focuses on consulting for large companies in need of business consulting. The topics of consulting that COMATCH concerns itself with are Startup Business Solutions, Management, Information Technology, Market Research, Operations and Strategy, and Finance. To work with COMATCH, you must have some business knowledge, but you may have some of this experience if you are a musical entrepreneur.

COMATCH works with large companies that submit a business proposal outlining their project and what type of consulting they require. From here, consultants are selected based on their knowledge of and experience with the project specified. The company can then choose between the submitted consultants by interviewing them over the phone or simply deciding on the best match. A contract is signed, and the consultant can begin working on the project. The platform itself is in charge of invoicing and recording all logistics to ensure that you are paid what you are owed. Your income possibilities will vary depending on your experience and the number of projects you are selected for based on how closely your skills match the current projects. It is difficult to estimate compensation as the company must first put you through their hiring process.

COMATCH began as a company in Germany but has quickly spread worldwide, including the United States. If you have skills and experience in business and would like to put these skills to use as a freelance, remote consultant, you can do so through COMATCH. Their hiring process is a little more stringent than the others, but it comes at a good price when it is time for payday. This company employs its consultants on a full-time basis. COMATCH allows artists or any other people to pursue their art (or other endeavors) while still making enough money to live well.

Independent Business Consulting

A business consultant focuses on helping business owners assist and guide them to run their business by clarifying their company's vision and how it aligns with their personal goals.

Alternatively, business consultants can help people looking to start their own business (entrepreneurs) and help guide them to follow the best business practices and help them create a vision for what they want their business to be. In simpler words, business coaches follow a process to help grow a business from its present state to where the client wants their business to be.

An essential part of business consulting is for the consultant to help the client understand that their company's vision and story are entirely theirs to create. Business consultants don't help their clients by creating their businesses for them; instead, they help them discover their business model and plan to execute it.

A business consultant's main role is to introduce concepts, tools, and processes to their clients that help them grow their organization and team to create a good, lucrative business. Here are a few other responsibilities of a business consultant:

- Optimize the alignment of the entire organization
- Increase accountability within teams and individuals in the organization
- Strengthen the company culture
- Increase the focus of the organization
- Make better decisions regarding the 'people.'
- Develop strategies that are more effective in growing the business

A business consultant can target individual clients, group clients, or corporate clients. In most cases, business consultants aim to market their services to corporate clients, as that is where they can bill the most hours at the highest rates. However, there are still a plethora of clients that fall into the individual category. Most of the time, these are people who have already started their small to medium-sized businesses and are looking to grow them further. They could also be people that do not have their own business yet, but who wish to build their own. In both of these cases, the business consultant helps assess what the client's current state is in terms of their business and helps them plan execution to grow their business to the place they want it to be.

Depending on what type of client the business consultant has, they could deliver their sessions in-person, over the phone, or by video conferencing. Most corporate companies that hire business consultants would require them to come into their workplace to deliver these sessions. In contrast, entrepreneur type clients may deem over the phone sessions sufficient.

Business consultants typically have some sort of background or career within the specific field that they are consulting on. This can range from having run their own business before having worked in management or executive-level positions in the business field. A business consultant must have a good grasp of how businesses work and how to grow them in size, revenue, and overall vision.

Like I mentioned earlier, there isn't a specific prerequisite for any type of consulting. It is important that you can assess yourself and see where your strongest skills lie to help you determine what consulting niche makes the most sense for you. Some business consultants specialize within the entrepreneur realm only, while others will take clients that are established companies.

Online Freelance Jobs

When it comes to freelance work, there are a plethora of different types. You could do freelance work in whatever skill or profession you already have. For instance, you could do freelance work in writing music for productions or advertisements if you are a musician or do some freelance English teaching if you are an academic. Further, if you have other skills like writing or manual labor, you can pick up jobs online and make perfect money through numerous projects.

The benefit of freelance work is that you don't necessarily have to stick to one skill set. Using the numerous freelance work platforms available nowadays, such as Fiverr.com, Upwork.com, Freelancer.com, Peopleperhour.com, Writeraccess.com, and Freelancewriting.com, you can find side gigs that are suitable for your range of skills. When it comes to freelancing, you can pick up as many or as little gigs as you'd like and schedule them around your music. These websites above offer freelancers multiple different ways to make money. You could act as a ghostwriter and help people write books on topics you know about, or you could help a YouTube artist create background music without copyright for their channel, or you could simply help someone run a specific errand and get paid for it. The world is yours, and you can choose whatever suits your skills best. Below are a few examples of what freelance work encompasses.

Online Freelance Platforms

Fiverr.com

Fiverr.com is a platform that connects freelancers with specific skills to clients that require them. Most of the freelance skills on this website are more tech-related, including logo design, WordPress, social media, SEO, and illustrations. If you have experience in design and in technology (e.g., programming), then a lot of this work will be relevant to your skillset. They also offer different categories of skills, such as translation, data entry, book covers, and voice-overs. This could be a great way for you to build a freelance business.

Upwork.com

Upwork.com is a platform that is similar to Fiverr that connects freelancers with specific skills to clients or agencies that require them. The categories that are included in Upwork are broader than Fiverr and include; Web, Mobile and Software development, Design & Creative, Writing, Sales & Marketing, Admin Support, Customer Service, Data Science and Analytics, and Engineering and Architecture. Some of these categories may require you to have the education and professional experience, but the categories such as Writing and Customer service may not. Any individual or agency can post freelance work gigs on Upwork.com to find the right person to fulfill their needs. This opens it up to big companies that may be looking to hire someone for multiple projects that require the same skillset. Most of these gigs are all done remotely, so you can still maintain a flexible schedule and working environment, which will allow you to keep working on your music.

Freelancer.com

Freelancer.com is similar to Upwork and Fiverr in the sense that it connects freelancers with specific skills to certain projects that require them. The most popular projects that freelancer.com receives include; website development, graphic design, Logo design, marketing, writing, and mobile app development. However, they have a huge selection of less popular categories but still have numerous projects posted daily. If you have any marketing experience or create logos, you may find projects that require those skills and apply to pick them up with this experience.

They also offer writing projects on this platform, so if you have experience writing articles, blogs, or e-books, this is the place to go to see what types of projects are available. Projects can range from $100 to over $500 + depending on the project size and skill type.

Peopleperhour.com

Peopleperhour.com is similar to the above platforms as it connects freelancers to projects and businesses that are looking for a certain skill. The most popular projects on this platform include video shooting experts, Go developers, Children book illustrators, appointment setters, Swift developers, Visual merchandisers, Arabic translators, interior designers, music composers, and wealth managers. As you can see, music composer is a part of their most popular categories – this may be right up your alley.

Tons of businesses and individuals are looking for people who can compose songs that they can use for their advertising or videos without copyright, so it doesn't get taken down on popular platforms like YouTube. Moreover, if you have experience shooting videos at concerts or if you know any other languages, you could look into those projects as they are popular on this platform. Specific to music composing, freelancers on this website are charging anywhere from $30 - $100+ per hour to compose original music.

Writeraccess.com

Writeraccess.com is different from the platforms that we just talked about as it is specific to writing, and you need to apply and get approved before you are matched with opportunities. If you are a strong writer and have experience writing blogs, books, articles, or e-books, then this is right up your alley. The genres of books offered on this site are endless as they have writers who can write about anything from agriculture to politics. For example, if you have special knowledge in a certain industry, you can use it to your writing advantage.

Freelancewriting.com

Freelancewriting.com is a platform that matches freelance writers to specific companies and individuals that require their services. The freelance work that is offered on this platform include; copywriting, content writing, project management, digital media management, SEO, RFP writing, and marketing. Writers can apply to these projects for free, while companies and individuals who seek these skills pay a fee to utilize their platform to find the right talent. All of these jobs are done from the comfort of your home so that you can maintain your flexibility in terms of hours and location.

Editing and Proofreading

Suppose you are someone that has good writing and editing skills. In that case, proofreading and editing written documents is a great way for you to make some extra income. This is ideal for someone who may be in the field of writing and is looking to increase their own writing skills while making money at the same time. There isn't a single platform that is dedicated to this type of work, but with a quick google search, you can find a variety of freelance proofreading and editing gigs. You can usually make around $200 - $300 per written document depending on its length, so just proofreading a few documents per month can significantly increase your monthly income.

Temporary Side Gigs

In this section, we will be focusing solely on a type of side gig that is temporary and on an hourly basis. However, temporary side gigs are easily confused with the remote jobs side gig as those are also paid on an hourly wage basis.

The main difference here is that temporary side gigs require you to be on the job site in person, while remote gigs are done entirely from your own home. Although this type of work is not as flexible as remote gigs, it opens up to many more skillsets than remote work. Remote work is mainly limited to people within the technology field and business administration field, while hourly/temporary gigs could be anything from bartending to customer service. For instance, if you have experience working in restaurants and bars, you can advertise those skills on platforms catered to this type of work. Employers who require temporary service staff could reach out to you and hire you for a temporary gig. The main platforms used to connect freelancers to companies and individuals that require services include shiftgig.com, appleone.com, and Wonolo.com.

In terms of earning potential for temporary side gigs, you can expect at least the minimum wage requirement based on where you live. Depending on what types of jobs you get hired for, you have the potential to earn tips as well. People in positions like servers, bartenders, and baristas have the potential to make a lot of extra money just on tips alone. This is a reliable type of income as you will be guaranteed money for the number of hours you put in. Let's take a look at a few platforms that support this type of work.

Shiftgig.com is one of the most popular platforms for employers to seek out temporary/hourly employees for their business needs. The most commonly sought-after jobs on this website include; bartenders, servers, cooks, housekeepers, porters, call-center representatives, customer service representatives, warehouse packers, retail specialists, promo models, and brand ambassadors. In terms of flexibility, this type of side gig is not as flexible as remote jobs and project-based work. Employers will set the time you need to clock in and clock out just like any regular job, and you must abide by those hours. However, you are guaranteed an income for the number of hours you put in, unlike setting up your online store or course creation, where your income highly depends on how many people purchase your services and goods.

Moreover, once you do an excellent job for a specific employer in this field, there is a high likelihood that they will contact you again for their next business requirement. Many restaurants and coffee shops that do pop up stores during conferences shows and fairs need a temporary set of staff during their busy times of the year. Again, the earning potential is average here as the minimum amount you will be paid the minimum wage in your area, but specific jobs that require skills higher than entry-level can be paid from $20 or more.

The next platform you can look into is appleone.com, where it acts as a recruitment platform for employers to seek talent for the temporary work that they need. This platform supports virtually any type of job out there and is not specialized in anything in particular. Some recruiters work for this platform that reaches out to the applicant base to contact people who meet the employer's requirements. Just like shiftgig.com, the flexibility is not as great as other side gigs as you need to be at your workplace at the requested clock in time and clock out at your set time as well. However, the income will be steady as you would be working any regular job but just on a temporary and hourly status. The number of hours you put in will equal the amount that you get paid.

The next platform we will be taking a look at is Wonolo.com. This platform is similar to shiftgig.com but is a little more specialized in terms of what types of employers and employees it's looking for. They typically specialize in warehouse operations, general labor, delivery drivers, food production, event staffing, washing, cleaning, administrative, and merchandising. They pre-screen candidates and allow them to create a profile on the platform, and they get matched with opportunities that employers post. The earning potential is relatively high with Wonolo as the pay rates range from $15 per hour to $20 per hour, depending on what your skillset is. It has the same flexibility level as the two other platforms we just learned about. Still, Wonolo is one of the biggest platforms in temporary/hourly staffing, so that you may find the most opportunities there.

If you have a range of skills or are simply just okay with doing some manual labor work, you can easily find gigs on Wonolo to help you pay your bills.

Overall, temporary/hourly side gig work is not much different than having a part-time job. The only difference is that you have more flexibility regarding when you can pick up work, but you still have to follow the employer's schedule based on their needs. If you have a reasonably flexible schedule and can physically be on a job site for a few days a week, this is one of the safest and most reliable sources of income out there. Remember, you can take on multiple side gigs at once to create different sources of revenue. You can be running an online store while picking up some warehouse working shifts to generate cash flow. Don't be tunnel-visioned, and make sure that you have more than one stream of income at all times.

Chores

This type of side gig is one of the newer ones that emerged over the last couple of years. Platforms like TaskRabbit allow people to list a range of tasks/chores/errands they require help with and are willing to pay other people to do it for them. This can range from running simple errands like picking up some things from the grocery store to assembling their IKEA furniture to helping someone make home improvements. This can make you a good amount of money if you have some useful life skills that you could charge money for. For instance, I hate building furniture, so I would happily pay a handy person a fair price to build my furniture for me. The average reported monthly income for TaskRabbit is around $110, which isn't a lot but could be an interesting side hustle for you to complement with others.

Cleaning

Similar to the above side gig, cleaning is another good option. Cleaning as a side gig is something anyone can do as long as you are someone who gains the satisfaction of turning a messy/dirty place into a clean and sparkling one. There is nearly no start-up cost, as most clients who hire this type of service provide the cleaning equipment and supplies. However, in the scenario that you are required to bring your own tools, they are cheap, and you likely have them in your own home already. Depending on where you live, there can be many people seeking cleaning services or not many at all. In big metropolitan cities where it's condominium and apartment galore, there are tons of clients that are seeking reliable and trustworthy cleaners to come in a few times a month to keep their place tidy. Moreover, if you live in a dense city, there are always renters and tenants moving in and out of homes, which opens up the market for landlords to hire cleaning staff to clean units before somebody new moves in.

You can find this type of work using websites such as Tidy.com, taskrabbit.com, and craigslist.com. You can even simplify this further and create your own ad on your local buy/sell groups offering your cleaning services at an hourly rate. You can offer different types of services related to cleaning at different prices. For instance, a routine weekly/monthly cleaning can be charged less than a yearly deep clean. You can also reach out to Airbnb owners and offer them your services as they need a cleaning person to come and remake units when the clients check out. Tidy.com helps clients get matched with home keepers and cleaners in their area; this includes Airbnb owners as well. Depending on what type of client you find or the agency that connects you, most cleaners make around $25/hour (2 – 3 hours per clean) or $100+ per unit cleaned. Those rates are specific to cleaning apartments and condominiums, but house cleaning wages start at $25/hour (4+ hours per clean) or $200 per unit.

Although Tidy.com, taskrabbit.com, and craigslist.com are good places to start looking for cleaning side gigs, you can research your own cleaning companies based out of your local neighborhood. Suppose you want to maximize your earning potential and not have to give a cut to any agency or company. In that case, you can build your own service and post flyers in local condominiums and apartments the old fashioned way to generate business. This type of work is ideal for those who enjoy cleaning and don't have the time to work for more than a few hours at a time. The scheduling is also quite flexible, so you can choose to schedule cleaning for your clients when you are not practicing music.

Moreover, this type of side gig is fairly reliable as once you do good work for a few clients, they'll likely routinely hire you every single week and month to upkeep their home. If you clean three units a week at $25/h, and it takes you about 2 hours per session, then you are making $150 per week and $600 per month. This is good money considering you only worked 6 hours per week!

If you believe cleaning and home-keeping are right up your alley, my recommendation would be to start off cleaning through an agency or platform like tidy.com to gain some experience and refine your skills. They pay reasonable rates, but you could make more if you went completely independent. Once your skills have been refined and you are 100% sure that this is the perfect side gig for you, I advise you to open up your own cleaning business and open up your client base to cleaning for move-in/move-outs for condos and houses, Airbnb checks in/check out cleaning, deep cleaning services, and weekly/monthly routine up-keeping. By establishing your own business, you build credibility with your repeat customers and guarantee yourself a steady income with a set client base.

Organizing
Organizing is a great side gig for those who find joy in keeping tidy and neat. Organizing side gigs can range from helping people sort out the junk from their home to organizing someone's pantry to installing fixtures or furniture in someone's home. If you are reasonably handy and comfortable with tasks that require manual labor, you may find yourself enjoying side gigs within the home organization field. Don't get mixed up; however, these jobs aren't solely just organizing people's homes; it goes as far as helping others remove tree limbs from their lawn or pressuring washing someone's desk or

backyard. Most of these side gigs do require you to have your equipment but very minimally. For instance, you can do all organization tasks with just your hands, so there is no start-up cost there, but if you are helping someone set up a new table or bookshelf, you may need to bring your toolbox.

Platforms that help connect clients with people who do this type of work include Takl.com and Thumbtack.com. Takl.com focuses more on side gigs related to someone's home or property, while thumbtack.com opens it up to people who may need help with other locations that aren't just limited to their homes. For instance, Takl.com already has a list of providers (people who are doing this for side gigs) that are ready to get paid for doing tasks like; mowing the client's lawn, cleaning their homes, hanging a light fixture, hauling away old appliances, mounting a TV, reorganizing furniture at home, cleaning out gutters, installing curtain rods and cleaning outside areas of a person's home.

If you register yourself as a provider and list all the skills you have, this platform can help you match yourself with clients requiring your assistance. This is especially good for someone who has a broad range of skills but not necessarily one primary talent with a large client base. For instance, you may be someone who is handy but is also good at cleaning. Instead of limiting yourself to platforms that are solely specialized in either space, Takl.com can help match you with every job related to every skill you have. Moreover, the scheduling is quite flexible with Takl, so you can schedule projects and clients whenever you are available. If your other job requires you to be flexible in terms of your schedule, you will find this helpful as you can plan your clients around your availability. Moreover, depending on your past job experience, you may have experience hauling equipment to and from locations, so moving around some furniture to help clients reorganize their living room should be an easy task and a quick way to make some cash.

It's hard to precisely identify the earning potential with Takl because it depends on what skill sets you are bringing to the table and what the clients are willing to pay. However, you can likely expect $20 per hour for most tasks, but they can also pay per project.

Thumbtack is a similar platform to Takl, but it opens it up to more services that are catered to different businesses and people rather than specializing in residential homes. Thumbtack helps clients connect to people like you that have experience in home remodeling (tiling, flooring, general contracting work), home maintenance (cleaning, painting, handymen), weddings (photographers, wedding officiants, makeup artists), events (caterers, DJs), interior design, lawn work, and roof repair and maintenance. If you are creative, you may be able to try your luck at DJ gigs that pay a reasonable amount if you have experience with that type of work. Thumbtack is a suitable medium for taking your side gig work and building it into your own side business. If you have the right certifications, skills, and equipment, you can undercut many professional companies when it comes to contracting work and weddings.

Some people have reported starting earnings to be between $500 - $1000, picking up projects paying over $3000 per month in terms of earning potential. Again, it highly depends on what your skills are and what equipment you have available. Still, if you develop a desirable skill within contracting and maintenance, you can make some serious cash.

Takl.com and Thumbtack.com are platforms that offer fantastic resources to people who are interested in a side gig. The highest-paying jobs are the ones that require handy skills like tiling, painting, and maintenance. If you know your way around different cables and connectivity, this would be an excellent choice for you. If this is the side gig route you want to go, start practicing your handy skills by picking up smaller home-projects on Takl.com, and you can move on and pick up more extensive projects and open up your client and project base on thumbtack.com. Remember, skills that require training like tiling and maintenance work are expensive for people to purchase at a commercial level. By learning these types of skills and refining them, you will find a lot of business in these areas if you slightly undercut those businesses.

Depending on what projects you pick up from these websites, they can range from being reasonably flexible to highly inflexible. For instance, if you pick up a kitchen tiling job, you likely have to work 1 – 2 full days to get it done as the client would not want the tiling to go on for more than a few days due to inconvenience. Needing these two days means that you would need 1 – 2 entire days off from your regular work to complete these projects. However, if you were picking up projects like pressure washing a deck or installing a light fixture, these jobs will be done in a few hours, and the client can be more flexible regarding when you can come and go.

Chapter 8: Property Rentals

This chapter will expand on our chapter five discussion of trading and investment options. This chapter will look at property rentals and real estate investments and how you can make quick, passive income from these.

Managing a property rental is a great option for a side gig. This method is perfect for someone who has an extra property or an extra room in their house/apartment. Various property rentals can earn you passive income, including long and short-term rental agreements. We will look at examples of each below.

Long-Term Rentals

The first type of income that you can earn from renting property is by being a Landlord. To do this, you can list a room, a house, or an apartment on any rental site, like craigslist, and find a tenant to rent your place by making monthly payments for a yearly contract.

Being a landlord allows you to make passive income by simply collecting rent payments every month. This method is a great, hassle-free, and hands-off way to make passive income. This is arguably the best way to make additional income because it allows you to pursue other endeavors like owning a business or working a day job while making rental income without putting in much effort. The only time that you would be required to earn your income actively is when your tenants need something or when you need to find tenants to rent actively. Once you sign a 12-month contract with your tenants, however, you do not have to do much else.

Short-Term Rentals

Vacation rentals

Vacation rentals are a growing form of side-hustle, especially for people who live in high-rent cities like New York City, San Francisco, or Toronto. You can make vacation rentals a larger source of your income if you have a spare room in your home or a property that you can fix up to be rented.

Renting out your room/unit on a nightly basis can make you anywhere from $50 - $250 per night. Some people decide to rent a room in their apartment from Friday – Sunday, as most people use the weekend to have a getaway. This method allows you to maintain your vacation rental property away from your day job while making anywhere from $150/weekend to $600/weekend. You also have the flexibility of setting your nightly price, so dates with higher demand like Christmas or Spring break can be listed at a higher nightly price.

Airbnb

Instead of paying rent or mortgage to your home while you are away, you can list it as an Airbnb or HomeAway rental for tourists or travelers to rent. Due to the increasing cost of nearly everything, people nowadays prefer to book an Airbnb compared to a hotel to save money by having the amenities to cook their food and fit more people into one space.

Event Space Rentals

Another side gig that is a great source of passive income is to rent out event space. This way, you collect a fee for people who want to use your space to host events such as parties, weddings, or anything else. This passive income source can make you a lot of money with very minimal work required on your part.

Commercial Property Rentals

If you can afford to buy a commercial property, you can rent it out to someone who wants to use the space to run a business. This kind of property requires more money upfront than a traditional house purchase, but it can provide you with great rewards in the long-run if you can hold onto it and collect rental income. This kind of property has the potential to provide you with the job of a full-time landlord if you can make enough income from it.

Rental Property Income Potential

If you are renting out a room or a unit in a house, you could easily charge upwards of $50 per night. This depends on where you live, as you must match your rate to the market value in the city or general location where your house is located. In some places, people charge up to $250 per night. With this range, your income potential could amount to a weekly income of $150 - $750 if you rent a space in your own home from Friday – Monday. Of course, if you rent an entire house or cottage, you can get more money per night, depending on how many rooms the house has. People can charge up to and beyond $600 USD per night in the most desirable locations for people to vacation. If you can manage to fill your month by having back-to-back rentals, this could bring you upwards of $18000 before Airbnb fees come out (if that is the platform you choose). As you can see, the income potential comes with a vast range of values, so it is difficult to say exactly how much you could make.

Buying and Selling Property

As I mentioned, renting a property is one great way to turn an investment property into a passive income source. In addition to providing you with income, it could also cover your mortgage payments for you while you wait for your house's value to grow. When this happens, you can sell, and you will make a lump-sum of money that you earned passively.

Tips for Investing in Income Properties

As I mentioned, investing in a property is a great and secure way to grow your money in the long-term. If you are in a position to buy a property, I strongly suggest it. Even if you are not ready to live in a property that you own, there are numerous ways to turn this into a passive income source for yourself. One way to turn this into passive income is by using it as a rental property. Doing this can bring you rental income or cover your mortgage payments for you. The second way is by simply investing your money and waiting for your house's value to grow. When this happens, you can sell, and you will make a lump-sum of money that you earned passively.

It can be challenging to make enough money to invest in a property, but any of the side gigs in this book can help you to earn and save passive income that will bring you closer to buying a property. For example, if you had enough money for a down payment for a property, think $50,000 - $100,000 at least, then you could invest in a home and turn it into a property where it generates rental income for you. Let's say you got a decent mortgage from your local bank, and you put down a $50,000 down payment for a $300,000 home. Now let's say you agreed to a monthly payment of $2,500 to your bank plus a 2.5% interest rate for ten years, which leads you to pay around $2560 a month. Since property prices tend to increase with time depending on where you live naturally, it's safe to say that your $300,000 investment could become a $400,000 investment in a few years. If you rent out your new property to tenants that cover the full mortgage ($2560), this means that you are no longer making payments to the bank, the tenants are, and you get to keep your money growing on your property. By spending $50,000 on your down payment, you are generating over $300,000 of income over the next few years with a high likelihood of it becoming a property that is worth way more than $300k in a few years. Let's say in 5 years your property value has increased to $450,000. By doing nothing at all, you have paid off $125,000 ($2500 per month x 5 years), and the value of your house has grown by $150,000. Therefore, in just five years, with minimal work, you have made $275,000. For some people, that is a decent salary of $55,000 a year for five years. All of this was made by simply having enough resources to build a strong passive income stream.

How to Choose a Property Type
In this section, I will break down the different types of real estate investment properties so that you can decide which is the best option for you.

Rental Properties
As discussed previously, this is one of the most popular forms of real estate investment. This kind of real estate investment is when a person buys a property intending to hold onto it and rent it out for rental income. This property could include a condo, a house, an apartment complex, or a building used as an event space.

House Flipping
House flipping is another option for investing and making quick money through real estate, but this method requires skill and expertise.

To do this, some people invest in real estate by purchasing a house for little money, fixing it up for as little cost as possible, and quickly selling it at a much higher price than purchasing it. This kind of real estate investment provides people with quick lump sums of profit, but it requires them to be build-savvy and work quickly, under pressure.

Real Estate Investment Groups

This kind of real estate investment involves a small mutual fund that purchases rental properties. People can then purchase units or apartments from the company that purchased the entire property. Once a person has purchased a unit or several units, the company in charge of the property will rent them to tenants. In this case, the real estate company will take care of all logistics involved in renting a property, from advertising to maintenance and everything in between.

Which Kind of Property Can Make the Most Income?

Below you can see which real estate investment properties are the most lucrative, which will help you choose which type of property you should invest your money into.

Commercial Real Estate

Commercial real estate includes a variety of different commercially available spaces such as:

- Office space
- Industrial space
- Parking spaces and parking lots
- Retail space
- Restaurant and service industry space
- Etc.

Commercial real estate involves renting to businesses, which is generally a smoother process than renting to individuals for residential purposes. Further, as a commercial landlord, you can charge much higher prices, especially if your space is in a highly desirable location.

Residential Rental Real Estate

Residential real estate is the second most desirable type of rental property. This kind of investment involves renting your property monthly to an individual every month, collecting rent, and acting as the landlord. This kind of rental can offer high income, as the tenants can pay your mortgage while your property value increases.

Properties For Flipping

The third most lucrative kind of real estate investment is the "fixer-upper" or the house flipping type of investment. This kind of investment can provide you with quick income. Still, it relies on your ability to work quickly and efficiently and your ability to fix up and renovate the property according to code and potential buyer's preferences.

Benefits of Property Income

It can be challenging to make enough money to invest in a property, but any of the side gigs in this book can help you to earn and save passive income that will bring you closer to buying a property. However, compared to other forms of investments, real estate is said to be one of the most reliable and secure. This kind of investment is great for those who are risk-averse and have the money to invest in a tangible, reliable investment. For this reason, if you can afford to buy a property, you will see returns on your investment.

Notes for Success

Now that you understand a little more about what real estate investment entails and how it can benefit you in numerous ways, I will share some tips for success in this realm of investing.

Plan Ahead

When investing, it is important to plan ahead in every sense of the word. Plan ahead when it comes to your money, your responsibilities, your risks, and your finances.

Research the Market

Before investing, it is important to research the market to make informed and educated decisions regarding your properties, buying, and selling. Be sure to look at projections for the future.

Maintain ethical investing standards
While you may get by using illegal or unethical tactics in real estate investing, this will not bring you long-lasting success. Since you are looking for early retirement, you want a plan that you can follow for years to come, so stay ethical.

Find a niche for yourself.
As we discussed in this chapter, there are various real estate niches that you can focus on. Find one for yourself and work up to becoming a boss in that niche.

Always keep yourself up-to-date.
You must stay up to date when using investing as a main source of your income. Don't sleep on the current statistics, market trends, or any other world events. Keep yourself informed.

Know the risks you are taking
As with any type of investing, you must know and evaluate the risks at each step of the way. Ensure that you know what risks you are taking before you take them.

Hire a Team of Professionals
You don't have to be an expert in every part of the real estate investment process. You will thank yourself later. On that note, don't be afraid to hire an entire team of professionals to help you at every step of the process. It will cost you some money, but it will pay off in the long run if things are done the right way and in a timely manner.

Find a mentor
Find yourself a mentor whom you can trust; it will make this process much smoother for you.

Chapter 9: Online Teaching and Coaching

This chapter will explore quick money-making methods that involve education, teaching, and tutoring. In our modern society, there is more than one way to learn a certain topic. Popular subjects like language, especially English, are often taught by people in America, Canada, and Europe to people from other countries who want to learn English. Moreover, online tutoring and in-person tutoring are a popular income method, especially centering on topics like math, science, and language studies. As long as you have some post-secondary education, you will qualify for most online teaching and tutoring jobs, and they can prove to be a great way to make quick money!

Tutoring Platforms

Let's talk a little about tutoring first, as this is the least intensive side gig in this chapter. Tutoring is an amazing side gig that can bring you a significant amount of income. You can find these opportunities through independent tutoring companies or online platforms like Wyzant and GlassGap.

Tutoring can be done in-person or online, depending on your preferences. Online tutoring is more flexible as you can do it from your home. Online tutoring is essentially the same as in-person tutoring except for the fact that you are doing it over video chat rather than sitting face-to-face. With online tutoring, the possibility of subjects widens even more. Now you have different options like teaching multiple languages or other subjects that may differ from what your local tutoring schools are teaching. Some of the most well-known tutoring platforms include tutor.com and pearson.com.

Depending on your education level, you could tutor students in elementary, high-school, and post-secondary schools. The higher the education level you teach, the higher you will get paid on an hourly basis. You can look at some online tutoring opportunities by looking them up based on where you live or starting with the online platforms that I will discuss below. If there are many high schools or well-known universities in your area, the chances are that many businesses or families are looking to hire tutors for various subjects. Moreover, if you have specific skills in a given area, you can also look into businesses looking to hire online teachers or tutors in that area.

The above options are highly dependent on where you are located, so you can spend your own time researching which options exist in your city. Let's take a look at each platform and see what they have to offer.

Tutor.com

Tutor.com is a large platform that offers tutoring services in pretty much every subject imaginable. The subjects that they cover include:

- o Math (everything from algebra to calculus to statistics to middle-grade math)
- o Science (biology, chemistry, physics)
- o English
- o Social studies
- o AP support (calculus, physics, biology)
- o SAT prep, foreign languages, and business.

In terms of earning potential, online tutoring does not pay as much as in-person tutoring because you need to go through an agency rather than finding clients on your own. Many tutors report making around $15 per hour using tutor.com, which is significantly less than tutoring in person. However, the flexibility is much higher, so you wouldn't need to leave the comfort of your own home, and you can build your schedule much easier.

Pearson.com
Pearson.com is a unique way to make money in the tutoring/teaching field. Rather than teaching students on various subjects, Pearson hires many online test-scorers to mark tests and exams. Virtually anyone can do this.

The one downfall to this is that the earning potential is much lower compared to teaching and tutoring. Most Pearson test scorers make anywhere from $12 - $13 per hour. However, you do get the benefit of working from home, so you get to enjoy your flexibility.

Lastly, since tests only happen at certain times of the year, there will be times where there isn't much to do, so this is not a steady side gig that can generate your income all year round. Tutoring and teaching can give you a steady flow of money throughout most of the year, but test marking and grading will only happen for a few months of the year, between September – August.

Language Instruction

As you are now aware, tutoring subjects can range from school subjects like math and science to teaching languages. English teaching is a quickly growing side hustle that can make you enough money to live on full-time.

VIPKid

VIPKid is an online English teaching platform. VIPKid pays its online English teachers anywhere from $17 - $22 per hour. The beauty of teaching English online is that you don't even have to leave the comfort of your own home, and you can choose which hours work for you. Meanwhile, tutoring can be done online or in-person, depending on which company you work for. If you are tutoring for a high school student, the average tutor gets paid anywhere between $30 - $40 per hour. Just by doing 10 hours of it a week can bring you $300 - $400 per week of extra income; that's $900 - $1600 per month.

Online Course Creation and Instruction

This type of side gig is a new addition to the world of side gigs and has increased in popularity over the last 1 – 2 years. These types of platforms offer courses to people who require them to qualify for jobs and further education. Platforms like udemy.com, teachable.com, and foundr.com offer courses that are made by other people at a discounted rate to either help people catch up on their credits or give them a certification that will allow them to qualify for their line of work.

Skillshare

Skillshare is an example of a platform that allows you to make passive income by simply creating courses for others to learn things you are passionate about. This platform is a great way to make money on the side, as you simply create a course, upload it and wait for people to purchase it. This way, you can sit back and make money once you create your course, and once it is completed and uploaded, you are finished. You can make as many or as few courses as you like, depending on how many areas of expertise you have. Skillshare is primarily focused on creative industries. For example, there are photography courses, graphic design, drawing, photoshop, animation, productivity, etc.

Thinkific
Thinkific is similar to Skillshare in that you create and upload courses, but Thinkific contains a much wider variety of course material. For example, sports and fitness, cooking, music instruction, business, marketing, and even things as specific as food photography. There is something for everyone on Thinkific, which is why this is a great option for people with niche skills or knowledge areas, especially if you have several different areas of knowledge that you can work with.

Udemy.com
Specific to Udemy.com, you can build your courses on virtually any topic possible and charge a price that you deem fair. You will get paid depending on how many people pay for your courses. Some courses are worth more than others, and people report to make anywhere between $1500 - $3000 per month for their work. This income is highly dependent on how much you promote your courses and how many people require this type of training. In some ways, if you are only selling your course work, I would say Udemy.com is a great

way to generate passive income because you won't have to do much after posting your course online for sale. However, it is not a reliable source of income as your pay will change drastically depending on how many purchases you get that month. I would keep this type of work as a source of passive income and have multiple other active income sources to generate the cash flow you need. This method definitely won't hurt to try out, especially if you already have course material at hand that you know inside and out. For instance, if you are a musician, you may know the basics of music and scales inside and out, so it will take you not much time to create a solid music foundation course.

Teachable.com

Let's talk a little about teachable.com. Teachable.com is a platform where a person can sell and create online courses for free. It allows you to build your own course website, host your content, and charge students interested in it for the course when they purchase it. Again, this is similar to Udemy as it's a great source of passive income because once you finish building your course, all you have to do is wait for it to be purchased. However, the business will heavily depend on your course's popularity and how many prospective students are in the realm of what your course offers. It is unknown so far for teachable in terms of earning potential due to the high variance from person to person. You can essentially make $0 if your course does not generate any students or interest, but some people have made over $18,000 in less than a month due to their course popularity. I'd like to drill in the point that this is a great way as a passive source of income but is highly unreliable if you want to make it your active side hustle source.

Foundr.com

Foundr.com is a resource aimed at people looking to build their own online business but need the guidance and knowledge others possess. Using the Foundr platform, you can make money by posting courses, articles, and teaching blogs about how one can jumpstart their own business. This platform isn't as popular compared to udemy and teachable due to its specialized nature. In Udemy and teachable, you can create and sell courses for virtually everything, while Foundr is focused on content related to entrepreneurship.

If you are a creative person, you may or may not have experience in this area. My recommendation would be to utilize the skills you already have through your previous education or your music skills, create courses that you're familiar with at ease, and put them up for sale as a type of passive income.

Create Your Own Course or Lesson Teaching Business

Another option you have that is similar to the above is to create courses that you can benefit from as a passive income source, but doing so without using a platform. That way, you won't have to pay fees to the platform to host your courses.

The challenge here will be finding clients to purchase your courses, but if you are confident that you can develop leads and find business, this could be a great option for you. You can do this by hosting courses on your own website and including a payment option.

Lessons

Now that we have covered all the in-person teaching options, let's look into some online music teaching platforms. The largest and most popular platform for this type of work is lessons.com. Lessons.com is specialized in music teaching and offers teaching in sports, dance, health, fitness, martial arts, cooking, driving, painting, and many more. As a teacher, you can post your subject of expertise and have students pay to sign up for your classes.

Lessons.com's earning potential varies a lot as it depends on how many people sign on to them. As a teacher, this platform allows you to contact potential students looking for specific lessons and send a quote for your services. This is mostly done online and is extremely flexible.

Online Coaching

This section will focus on another specific type of teaching or tutoring side hustle – coaching. To begin, I will explain what coaching entails. One way to become a coach is to start your own coaching business, where you act as both the coach and the administrator. In this business, you will need to find clients that you feel you can help.

Ideally, you must have a plethora of experience in the field of coaching that you are looking to specialize in. If you have been in the workforce for a while or have a good education, there is likely a niche of coaching that you would be suitable for. For instance, some people who found success working in a sales job may be interested in starting a business coaching side hustle. In comparison, someone who has found success as a Yoga teacher or enthusiast may be interested in starting a spiritual coaching business.

We will get more specific later in this section when we learn about different types of coaching opportunities. There are many different types of coaching businesses, and there is something for everyone; it is just a matter of finding out what makes the most sense for your knowledge and skills.

Most people hire a coach to help them with specific projects, transitions, or personal goals. The coach's responsibility is to help you grow by assessing your current situation, limiting beliefs, and other challenges. The coach will then create a customized plan that they design to help you achieve your goals.

If you are thinking about starting your own coaching business in the first place, you probably want to know how coaching compares to a career during these unstable times of the economy. The best part about this is that coaching is gaining an excellent reputation as a profession, probably because of the uncertainties in our economy, forced career changes, and businesses' drastic efforts to make their operations more efficient and productive during numerous financial challenges. In terms of statistics, the coaching industry in 2012 brought i2 billion spread amongst approximately 50,000 coaches.

You may already know that coaches set their rates and their rates tend to differ a lot. Some coaches may charge $25 per hour, while some may charge $300+ per hour. After coming out from a certification program, the standard hourly rates for certain coaches can be anywhere from $100 per hour to $150 per hour.

The most significant differentiating factor between coaching rates depends on the type of coaching that you are doing. Although there are numerous different coaching types, the industry includes life coaching, business coaching, and executive coaching.

A recent study on the coaching industry found that the average income for coaches who worked full time was over $80,000. For coaches who did it part-time, it brought in revenue of around $25,000 per year. For you to have a good understanding of what type of coaching brings in the most income, let's take a look at some of the top coaches in our industry today that are making over $100,000.

This section will learn about the different opportunities that exist if you are thinking of choosing coaching as your side hustle. There are many different types of coaching side hustles to choose from, and this section will help you narrow down your choices based on your experience and expertise.

Corporate/ Career Coaching

Career coaches are focused on helping people that are seeking career advice. These coaches use a very solution-oriented approach to help these people define, redefine, and achieve their goals related to their current working situation's professional objectives. For example, a career coach can help people figure out what type of job they're looking for next to grow their careers. They specialize in giving people advice based on what their current working situation is. They could be executives, employees, or freelancers. Regardless, career coaches help these people develop skills like leadership, stress management, self-confidence, interpersonal skills, and conflict-management skills. Depending on the clients' needs, the career coach's responsibilities, tasks, and services will differ accordingly, but the core coaching process is still the same in all cases.

Financial Coaching

A financial coach is responsible for helping their clients with money management basics. They work with clients struggling with their money management or those who simply have an unhealthy relationship with money. A financial coach's primary responsibility is to help their clients develop better and healthier money managing habits that are sustainable. Financial coaches spend a lot of time educating their clients on personal finance basics and work hand-in-hand with them to create a financial plan to help them achieve their personal goals. They also focus heavily on empowering their clients to be responsible for their spending actions and help them develop accountability for themselves.

Typically, financial coaches work with each client for several weeks. They would meet with their clients every week to advise them on their finances and check in on their progress.

The process that financial coaches use typically consists of three steps. The first step is to help them become more aware of their spending habits by tracking their spending to see for themselves. The second step is to help the client build their own financial goals, whether it's to pay off debt, save up for a property, or simply create a budget. The last step in this process is for the financial coach to help their clients build out sustainable plans and hold them accountable to follow those plans.

You might be wondering what the difference is between a financial coach and a financial advisor at this point. The main difference is that a financial coach helps teach those who aren't strong in money and finance management to better manage their money. In contrast, financial advisors advise you on growing and investing your money. Typically, financial coaches work with clients who don't have many assets and need to generate more financial stability for themselves. In contrast, financial advisors usually make their money by charging a percentage of the money your assets are generating. Financial coaches usually charge by the hour or have a flat retainer fee.

Financial coaching has the flexibility of being done in person, over the phone, or via video conferencing. The kind of meetings you hold is quite flexible as there isn't a need for the financial coach to see the client face to face. Since these sessions' purpose is to focus on money management, there isn't a need to be face-to-face.

If you think financial coaching is your niche, you may be interested in specializing in it even further. You could specialize your financial coaching services towards people looking to get out of debt or looking to save up for a down payment, or those who simply are bad with money. You can identify which further specializations are the most suitable for you by assessing your own experience. Have you ever experienced getting yourself out of debt? Have you ever saved up for your down payment? Or are you someone who used to be terrible with their money but now have multiple assets? These are all things you could consider before choosing what your coaching type will be.

Performance Coaching
Performance coaches are focused on helping clients who need to improve their performance or abilities for a specific task they have or want a career in, like sports. However, performance coaching helps both athletes and non-athletes alike.

For instance, writers can use performance coaches to get an idea of their full potential when it comes to writing. The performance coach can help assess where they are in terms of their writing skill, assess their work, and help guide the client toward creating a vision and a set of goals that can be accompanied by an action plan.

Performance coaching is one of those coaching types where it's almost necessary to specialize even further. Some performance coaches only coach people in the performing arts like ballet, while other performance coaches may focus on half-pipe snowboarding.

Performance coaches are responsible for facilitating conversations with their clients so that the clients are encouraged to set goals that are achievable and are working towards a larger goal. These coaches also help their clients build their self-awareness to identify and overcome any challenges and obstacles they may face when looking to improve their desired skills.

If you are looking to do performance coaching, it is ideal for specializing even further within a skill that you are confident you have a lot of knowledge. For instance, if you have been a snowboarder your whole life and want your side hustle to be performance coaching, it will be beneficial for you to advertise your coaching business as performance coaching specializing in snowboarding. Due to your history and experience with this sport, you can gain a lot of credibility when marketing your services and pitching your ideas to clients.

Performance coaching can be done individually, in groups, or in corporate situations. Most of the time, it is done individually, but corporate companies may seek out this type of service. For instance, dance studios or boot camp companies may seek out a performance coach to help their clients further build upon their skills.

Spiritual Coaching
A spiritual coach focuses on helping the client connect with their inner-self. These coaches help their clients change, navigate, and re-direct their lives to discover their desires, goals, dreams, and break out of any limiting beliefs. Unlike the other types of coaching we've discussed, spiritual coaching's main goal is to help people get in touch with themselves. A person may want to get in touch with themselves because they have lost their way in life and need to re-discover who they are. It could be someone who's gone through an impactful experience and want to explore new beginnings.

Spiritual coaches use a more holistic approach with their clients. They tend to help their clients discover their operating system that is under their consciousness. Spiritual coaches help people discover more than just who they are on the surface.

Spiritual coaching helps the client discover their depth and helps guide the client as they journey through self-discovery. All these changes run deeper than just surface level, but they all involve finding the underlying understanding of a person's being that contributes to long-lasting happiness.

Spiritual coaching can happen in person, over the phone, and via video conferencing. It can also be in the form of individual sessions, group sessions, and corporate sessions. Since spiritual coaches focus on everything below the surface, there isn't a need for sessions to happen in person, so normally sessions over the phone will suffice. If you think that spiritual coaching is your niche, you know what I'm about to say next – you can specialize even further. You can specialize in your spiritual coaching services to help people move on from trauma or help people break away from the norm and discover who their inner-self is. Remember, the best way to identify your second specialization is to look back onto your own experience and assess what areas you feel confident in coaching others.

Wellness or Nutrition and Fitness Coaching

Wellness coaches help their clients by assisting them in building sustainable and healthy behavior in their day to day lives. They do this by helping the clients identify their skills, strengths, and resources and help them create a vision of who they want to be and guide them towards it. This can include fitness coaching, nutrition coaching, or a holistic approach to wellness, depending on where your expertise lies and what your clients are looking for.

Like I mentioned numerous times, there isn't a prerequisite to becoming a coach. There is no prerequisite for becoming a wellness coach; anyone can do it as long as they are in a position where they can influence and help others through science-based tools. Wellness coaches help clients make changes to their present wellness. The clients can range from people who have a smoking or drinking habit to someone who is perfectly physically healthy but wants to improve their mental wellness.

Overall, course creation and instruction side gigs are beneficial to those who have a passion for teaching and are semi-skilled in course creation. This type of work gives the freelancer a great opportunity to make large sums of money, but there is a high-risk factor. If you put in 5 hours building your course for sale and you don't make any sales at all, then you just lost out on the time you put in when you could have used that time for other side gigs with a guaranteed return. As I mentioned throughout this chapter, it may not be the biggest income source if you use online course creations as your main income source. Instead, combining it with other sources and analyzing how well your sales are doing in the background before putting all your eggs in one basket may be better.

Keep in mind that flexibility is great in course creation gigs. Due to its nature, you can do this type of work anytime you want as long as you have a computer that will allow you to do so. There are no tight deadlines, and you can post courses for sale whenever you want. This option could be a very good option for a fairly busy creative who wants a passive income source to pay their bills.

Translation

If you are fluent in more than one language, you hold an extremely desirable skill to other people.

Platforms such as MotaWord and Unbabel help match multilingual people to clients that require their services. This is a side hustle that you can do from home or in person. Moreover, you can do these services, either translating words in real-time or translating written words like a book or an article. The income using these platforms ranges depending on the languages used and the type of work. However, many other companies or independent listings seek translation services if you are interested in this type of work.

Personal Trainer

This side hustle is also a very popular one and is so successful that many people have turned it into their main source of active income. If you are an ex-athlete or someone that is just well-versed in the world of fitness, you can make anywhere from $40 - $100 per hour training other people in the gym. This is even better if you are someone in the health and fitness field and can also use this side hustle experience to boost your own resume and career.

You can find clients in your own city by posting ads, or you can provide virtual training using platforms like GymGo. Keep in mind that most people like to work out in the mornings or after work, so your main working hours would likely be before 9 am or after 5 pm. If you train for 10 hours a week, you can make anywhere from $400 - $1000 per week, which is a monthly income of $1600 - $4000.

Chapter 10: How to Choose Which Income Source to Pursue

Side hustles are a great way to make extra money to pay off existing debt and to begin building a savings account that you can use to generate more money in the future. If you can accomplish these goals with passive income, while still working your day job, that is even better! This chapter will talk about how you can determine which secondary income source is best for you.

Considerations to Make Before Choosing

There are many different income sources to choose from; you can either build your own business or work on a freelance, contract, or on-call basis for another company. Some of these options are better suited to become passive income sources down the line, and some are better suited to become full-blown businesses down the line.

Keep in mind that a side hustle is different than a second job- as being employed as an "employee" simply means that you now have two jobs. However, picking up contracts or freelance work is a side-hustle because you get to choose how much you want to work and when you do it. Keep this in mind when choosing your secondary income source.

Take Stock of Your Resources

The first step in choosing a passive income source is to examine the resources you have access to. It is essential to talk about your current resources and examine whether you have enough resources to support the side job you are considering.

For instance, if you are interested in starting a business, you must be aware that it will not provide you with passive income right away, so you must make sure you have a secure day job that can support you while you get your side hustle going. Later in this chapter, we will discuss how you can transition from a day job to a full-time online income, but you must be aware that it will take time for now.

What are your Financial Resources?

If you have many resources to work with, it will be much easier for you to generate extra income. Have you ever heard the saying, "your first million is the hardest?" this is because money begins to make itself when you have enough of it.

If you are a person who has ample financial resources, you will likely be more interested in the financial realm of passive income, such as Stocks, Bonds, Commodities, and so on, or real estate income. If you have money to invest right now, you can essentially start making passive income immediately by investing it or beginning to trade stocks.

For instance, imagine you have a small fortune saved up, say $20,000. You can easily put that $20,000 into high-interest savings account at your local bank and generate 2-3% interest on it monthly. Doing this means that you are making $4,800 - $7,200 yearly by doing nothing at all. Although breaking it down into a monthly income, it's not much. That being said, simply just putting your money in a high-interest savings account can make you as much as any other new side hustle can. This method is the easiest way to make a passive income, but you could make even more money by doing other more elaborate things, such as buying a rental property or a car to rent out.

That being said, I understand that most people don't have $50,000 lying around to use as a down payment for a home, so I will spend most of this chapter talking about building a side hustle or a business that makes sense for you. Once this side hustle or business makes you enough money, then you can begin to invest it and grow it exponentially.

What are your Physical Resources?
The side gigs in this book will vary in terms of their individual start-up costs. Some may require you to invest in equipment or tools,

while others only require your body! Depending on your resources, you may qualify for more or fewer of these options.

For example, are you able-bodied? Do you have some physical resources available already, like a video camera, a car, a second property, a computer, or equipment to run a business of your choice? These resources will influence your choices for starting a side hustle. Moreover, depending on your resources, it will open up doors for your side gig options. For instance, if you have a car, you will qualify to do numerous side gigs requiring a vehicle. If you have a spare house or property, this opens up multiple options for you as well. However, if you are someone with very limited resources, you may have to stick to the side gigs that don't require much equipment.

What Skills do you Have?
The next step to choosing a side hustle or a passive income source is to examine your skills.

If you have the skill to start a side business, this will provide you with a higher earning potential than a side hustle that does not require any specific skills. It is beneficial to consider that option first when choosing a side hustle, as it is more suitable for your knowledge, skills, and income.

For instance, many different side hustles out there, ranging from blog platforms to teaching personal training. These side hustles require specific skills and have the potential to earn you an extra income of $500 - $4000 per month.

Use Matching Platforms

Numerous platforms aim to match people with specific side hustles based on work skills in our modern world. Thanks to these platforms, about 10% of people have a side hustle in American households today.

Capitalize on your Interests and Experience

Any time someone is spending time doing something they enjoy, they are more likely to succeed. For this reason, think about what you enjoy and which of your life experiences may lend themselves to that job.

Throughout this book, I described numerous side gigs and their earning potential, and I also described what type of person this side gig is most suitable for. This information will help you decide on whether or not this side gig is ideal for you. Read back on the side gigs that spoke to you the most and evaluate yourself to determine whether you would be a good fit for that side gig.

In the scenario that you have started a side gig that you don't enjoy or doesn't meet the earning potential you imagined, then I encourage you to try a few others. Finding the perfect side gig that you enjoy pays well, and that allows you to balance your time takes trial and error. Don't give up just because the first side gig you tried didn't meet your expectations, try something else, and keep at it until you find one that works for you.

Tips for Success

I want to note that to find success in your side gigs, don't silo yourself into just one specific side gig. You should always have at least two side gigs ongoing. This way, if one gig is slow in business, you can focus on you're the other one. Having only one side gig puts you at the risk of not being able to pay your bills if it's slow in business for one month.

Further, keep in mind that the different side gigs featured in this book vary in popularity and earning potential depending on where you are located in the world. For instance, San Francisco will have many side gigs due to the high-tech and populated city compared to rural areas with a low population. If you are located in a big city, then luck is on your side. Most of these side gig suggestions will apply to you and will likely have a large client base. However, if you live in rural North Dakota, some of these side gigs will not make sense. Keep this in mind as you decide which side gig may be best for you.

People cannot achieve their financial goals without using self-discipline.

People cannot achieve their financial goals without self-discipline, so make sure you supplement your goals with a self-discipline list. It will help you focus on the tasks and behaviors you need to perform to achieve your goals. For example, one of your goals is to save $2,000 in 6 months. Your discipline list will include putting aside at least $350 every month and avoiding spending money on unnecessary things like fancy restaurants or video games. High self-discipline in this example would be doing everything on that list without any exception. It does not mean that you cannot reward yourself or take a break from working towards your goals; it simply means that you should get the things done on your list before indulging in any rewards.

Use a daily list to track your finances and to monitor unnecessary spending.

Make sure you are using a daily list to keep track of all the things you need to get done to achieve your goals. Try to use online tools or just a simple notebook that can help you prioritize and organize. It feels very satisfying to check off items that you've completed, and it will even motivate you to finish other tasks that are on your list just to feel the satisfaction of being able to check off another box. Make sure your to-do list works hand-in-hand with your discipline list to help yourself stay on track. A useful tip to keep in mind when you're feeling unmotivated is to start with the easiest item on the list just to get the ball rolling. Once you complete one easy task, people normally feel more motivated than before; this will help you get started on the rest of your list. Starting with a harder task may create apprehension about doing it; therefore, start small and work your way up.

Figure out which obstacles are holding you back from success.
Different people have different things that distract them from being able to complete important tasks. For example, a person that is easily distracted by emails and people in their office might have to close their office door as soon as they get into work to get their tasks done. They may delay any phone calls or meetings unless they're necessary for completing their set of responsibilities. This method is effective for people that may be trying to lose weight. For example, if they know that junk food is their weakness, instead of resisting eating junk food in their house, they can simply eliminate all the junk food in their house, so they don't have access to it. You must minimize and remove all temptations of the distractions that affect you the most when reaching your most important goals.

Share your financial goals with other people.

It may be easier for some people to stick with completing a goal when they have made a public commitment. The thought of failing to reach a goal in front of other people can motivate them to stick with it. You can also take this one step further and ask those people to hold you accountable as well. If you aren't sharing your goals with anyone, nobody will know if you have been slacking off from it. When nobody is there to hold you accountable, you will likely be less motivated to keep doing it since nobody will know if you failed.

Use external sources or motivation as well as internal.
A saying goes, "don't do it for others; do it for yourself." However, some people find that they are much more disciplined when they know that their impulses, emotions, behaviors, and actions affect other people. Contrary to popular belief, it's alright to use external sources to help your motivation. Sometimes, motivation coming from external sources is more powerful than internal motivation. Find the purpose beyond yourself that is important to you to help give you a higher chance of success.

Discipline is created by creating habits.
When something becomes a habit, you no longer need to draw from your will power bank to get yourself to do it. For example, if your goal was to stop spending money at restaurants for lunch during the workday, get into the habit

of making yourself fulfilling meals to prevent yourself from buying food when you're at the office. You will be able to see the benefits of saving money if you can stick with it. Once you see the benefit, you will have more motivation to keep doing it, and soon it becomes a habit where it will feel strange not to make your meals. This way, you will no longer need to draw from your bank of self-control, but instead, meal-prepping will come naturally since it has become a habit of yours.

Stop making excuses.
Don't procrastinate, or wait for tomorrow, do it now. If you fall off the wagon, that's okay. Start over immediately. Stop telling yourself that something is too hard, or there's something that you cannot change. Don't blame other people for the circumstances that you're in. Making excuses is the Kryptonite of self-discipline. Achieve a mindset that is more about "I can do this" rather than "I'll do it tomorrow."

How to Balance Online Income and Your Day Job

As I mentioned at the beginning of this new endeavor, you will need to work to build your side hustle in the hours that you are not working your day job. Due to this, your working hours for your side hustle will likely take place during weekends, evenings, or holidays. This will be taxing at first, but it will quickly become worth it when you begin to see the extra income flowing into your bank account.

If you have goals that require a lot of money, like buying a property or investing in stocks to trade, then creating multiple sources of passive income on top of your active income may be the ideal route. For this reason, you will likely need to spend a lot of time outside of your day job working to build this sum of money. The good news is that once you have it, you can relax and watch as your money makes more money in the form of ROI. ROI stands for "Return on Investment."

Whether you are an investor or business owner, return on investment is an important analytical tool that you will need to use. The definition of ROI is the relationship between a loss and a profit, which will be important to you when you begin to invest or as you build your own business.

ROI is described as an investment. This number is always written or described as a percentage increase or decrease related to the fiscal year's investment value. Here is a simple example: imagine that you invest $200 on stocks, and the value of those stocks increases to $220 by the end of that fiscal year. In this example, your ROI would be 10%. In one more complicated example, if you invested $1000 in coffee bean stock for your coffee business and at the end of the year you generated $2200 from selling coffee made by the beans (assuming no other costs or taxes are involved), your ROI is 220%.

What this means is that you will need to put in a lot of extra hours to build that initial sum of money, but once you do, you will be able to watch as your investments grow that sum!

How to Transition From Your Day Job to Full-Time Online Income

Once you begin to make money from your side gig, or your second source of income, you can begin to scale back the hours you spend working your day job and transition to gaining your income from this side hustle alone.

Most people who start their side hustle still have to work a traditional full-time job simultaneously. The reason for this is because side hustles may not generate enough (or any) income until you get the proper traction and marketing to begin making money. Having a full-time job enables you to have the ability to pay your bills while also spending some of your free time building your side-hustle, so eventually, it does start creating a separate stream of income.

In the beginning, you will have two sources of active income, one is your day job, and the second being the income that you make from your side hustle business. However, you could turn your side hustle business into a passive income source if you can grow it to the point where you can employ other people to work for your business or offer services to your business. At that point, you can hire somebody else to manage your business functions, such as accounting and operations, and you can sit back and just collect the money as it comes in. At this point, it will become a passive income source for you.

Getting to the point of gaining passive income does take quite a bit of time, work, dedication, and luck. Still, if you want to develop a sustainable source of passive income without many resources, you will have to grow your side hustle until it is big enough to become a standalone business. At that point, it can begin to provide you with passive income.

Starting a side hustle business is a great way for you to start saving some extra money. This extra money will open up two options for you;

- The first option is to grow your coaching business into one that is big enough that it turns into a good stream of passive income.

- The second option is to grow your side hustle business into big enough where you can employ or contract other people to do the groundwork for you. What this means is that you will aim to reach a point when your side hustle business develops a reputation that is good enough for you to have a steady stream of business (or too much business for you to handle alone). At that point, you can begin hiring employees or contractors to work for your business. Hiring people is a good way to turn your side hustle business into a passive income source. If done properly, you would be able to hire someone to manage your operations and a team of people that work with your clients while you sit back and enjoy the flow of revenue.

One thing to keep in mind is that in between, as you grow your business, there may be a period where this becomes an active income source. There may come the point while growing your side hustle business when its income begins to exceed your current active income (your day job). At this point, you can comfortably replace your day job with your side hustle (aka, your side hustle becomes your day job). However, this would mean that your coaching business will not become a stream of passive income. If, though, you choose the second option instead, you can hire others to run your business while you continue your day job.

You ideally want to upgrade your passive income as you earn more money to eventually achieve one or several short-term goals that will help you meet your specific financial freedom goals in the future. Regardless of which option you choose, one of your interim goals should be to save up the money you make from your side-hustle to eventually build a strong stream of passive income. One example of a strong investment is investing in a property, for example, as this is one of the most secure and reliable investments to make. This investment can also help you develop even more passive income by doubling it as a rental property. In my opinion, the best type of passive income is some type of investment, whether it's in stocks, bonds, or property. We will discuss this further in this book, but guaranteed income (like an investment property) is the way to go if you are not risk-averse and just want to increase your overall income.

Chapter 11: Starting your Own Business

This chapter will look at a few final examples of ways to create a profitable online business. All of the examples in this chapter can provide you with quick, easy income as long as you have customers! It will take resilience and determination, but once you get your first client, you will feel great!

Examples of Quick, Profitable Online Businesses

Below are several examples of quick, profitable online businesses that you should consider starting. Some of them use online platforms, and some of them would require you to start a business and find clients from the ground-up.

Car Rental Businesses

Using your car to make extra money is one of the quickest and most reliable sources of income in the world of side gigs. The reason for this is its huge client demand, especially in major metropolitan cities.

Doing this work comes with many benefits, like building your schedule, which adds a ton of flexibility. Additionally, the income is very steady during prime hours like before or after work, Friday evenings, and weekends.

The earning potential is also quite high in this type of side gig; drivers report making anywhere from $11 per hour to $29 per hour. Factoring in its high level of flexibility and easiness of the job, that's great money! Let's begin to look at the various ways you could make money using your car.

The first way you can make a side gig out of your car is to rent your actual vehicle. It's just what you're thinking; you are essentially acting as a car rental company but only with your vehicle.

Using a car is a great passive source of income as you don't need to do anything besides confirming your customers, and you receive money from them using your car.

Unlike ridesharing gigs like Uber and Lyft, you don't need to put in the hours to generate income actively; as long as your car is in decent shape, you can make money just by letting someone else use it temporarily. This method is a great option for making good money by renting your car out if you don't use it a lot.

Platforms such as Getaround, Turo, and Hyrecar pay you money to rent out your car just like any car rental company would, and you essentially get paid for doing nothing at all!

Average car renters make anywhere between $500 - $800 per month renting out their car. If you rent it out 100% of the month, you will make more money than only renting it 50% of the time. The car model makes a difference, so if you have a fancy car like a Tesla, you can make a premium.

Turo
At the moment, it seems like Turo is the most popular platform in terms of car rentals, so that is one platform you can look into if you are interested in renting out your car. This platform also comes with a nice feature to estimate how much your specific make and car model can make for you. This feature is ideal if you want to estimate its income before diving right into this type of side gig. With its increase in popularity throughout major cities, especially those with high tourism, you can make some serious cash by just letting someone drive your car for a few days! Not only does this help you make some extra cash if you are currently financing or leasing your car, but you can also use this money to help break-even with your purchase. Two birds, one stone!

Getaround
Getaround is a similar platform to Turo in that it offers the same services. It does not have the same feature as Turo with the estimation calculator. Still, you could consider cross-posting your car into multiple car-share websites to maximize the number of times you can rent your car by maximizing your reach.

The earning potential is highly dependent on what type of car you have and the demand in your city, but most car-renters report making anywhere from $500 - $800 per month.

HyreCar
HyreCar is an interesting platform as it is a combination of Turo and Getaround mixed with Uber and Lyft. Its services are specialized towards people who don't have a car but want to pursue rideshare jobs. HyreCar allows people to rent Uber/Lyft qualified cars to use Uber and Lyft to make money. This platform is an option for you as well in terms of side gigs.

If you don't have a car, you can rent a car starting from $25 per day and generate income through rideshare or food delivery services. If you DO have a car of your own, you can make money by posting on HyreCar and renting it to someone else who wants to use it for Uber or Lyft to generate their income.

Again, if renting out your car is an option you are looking to pursue, cross-posting on these sites will help you generate the most business. Remember that renting out your car is a passive income. It allows you to do something else to make more money as a more primary and active source of money.

Starting Your Own Car Rental Business

The final option for renting your car is to create your own car rental business. If you have multiple cars that you don't mind renting out, you can create your own business. By doing it this way, you don't have to pay fees to a platform such as Turo or Getaround, but it will come with its own set of challenges. The great thing about using a platform like Turo is that the insurance for your renter is included. If you are planning on creating your own business, there will be many more logistical issues for you to look into, such as insurance, car storage, and so on. If you have ample resources at your fingertips, this could be a great option for you, but ensure that you look into everything involved before pursuing this option.

Food Delivery Businesses

Another very popular side gig these days that you can do with a car or some means of transportation is acting as a delivery service. People may need many different kinds of delivery services, but the most popular in today's world is food delivery.

Services like UberEats, Foodora, and Doordash frequently employ a team of food delivery people to pick up food from restaurants and deliver it to the person who ordered it. This type of side hustle originally started with delivering food from established restaurants but now have evolved into delivering everyday items like groceries, over the counter medicine, and alcohol.

If you own a vehicle or a bicycle and enjoy roaming through the city you live in, you can sign up and make some money doing so. The type of transportation you use will largely depend on your resources, but there is no shame in starting on a bicycle until you have enough money to buy a car. These couriers have reported that they make around $12 - $20 an hour. If you dedicate an extra 10 hours of your week to this side hustle, you can make an extra $120 - $200 per week, grossing $480 - $800 of extra monthly income. This method is not a passive source of income in any way, but it is a second active income that you can add to your earnings on your way to developing passive income.

Creating Your Own Delivery Business
If you have the means, you can create your own delivery business, which will allow you to make passive income. This delivery business could be a courier service, a food delivery service, or any other delivery service type. If you create a business like this, you can employ drivers and delivery persons, which will allow you to take a more hands-off approach and make passive income.

Dog Walking

This type of side gig is up and coming and is slowly increasing in popularity. If you live in a big metropolitan city, you likely know that most people are gone from 8 – 10 hours a day at their day job, leaving their pets with no one to look after them. This trend began the rise of dog walking in big cities. There are a few different ways that you can do this, including starting your own dog walking business or finding work through an online platform.

Companies like Rover employ contractors that love animals to help other people walk their dogs when they're not home. They also offer more passive services, like dog sitting or cat sitting, where you either take the person's pet into your own home and care for them while the owners are away, or you make drop-in visits to someone else's home to care for their pets (likely cats in this scenario).

However, when it comes to dog walking, the hours are usually during the day where other people at work. For this reason, this option wouldn't work as a side hustle if you are someone that works the regular hours of 9 – 5 (or somewhere around there).

However, you could work as a pet sitter as that requires slightly less involvement compared to dog walking. Dog walkers that do it part-time for about one week out of a month usually make around $1000, while pet sitters make around the same.

House Sitting
House sitting is a great side-gig as you can rent out your property while you are living somewhere else (and make rental income) while also getting paid for watching over someone else's home while they are away.

There are many platforms that can connect you with this kind of opportunity, like *House Sitters America* or *Trusted House Sitters,* that specialize in matching people who require house sitters to people who are interested in doing it. Another way to make money is by creating and running your own house-sitting business. You will need to find people who trust you to look after their house at the beginning, but once you build a reputation for yourself, you may find that many people want you to look after their house while they go on vacation. This is a great option if you don't mind moving from house to house, depending on where the business is.

Often, house sitting entails watering plants, bringing in mail, and keeping the person's home safe and clean throughout their trip. Although this type of side-hustle is not as popular as the ones listed prior, it is one that requires minimal effort, and you can incorporate other side-hustles (like renting out your own home while you are living at someone else's) to maximize your income.

Conclusion

As you can see, in today's world, there is an abundance of ways to make money, all you have to do is get creative, and you can find financial independence! I hope that this book has given you numerous ideas and places to turn for extra, quick money.

I challenge you to begin pursuing one or two of the side gigs in this book, and you will see for yourself how much potential there is out there!

Finally, if you like this book and recommend it to others, please leave us a positive review on Amazon! I appreciate you choosing this book, and your review would help me reach as many people as possible.